EARLY CHRISTIAN RHETORIC

AMOS N. WILDER

EARLY CHRISTIAN RHETORIC

The Language of the Gospel

HARVARD UNIVERSITY PRESS

CAMBRIDGE, MASSACHUSETTS

*To Colleagues and Students
in the Harvard Divinity School
1954–1963*

CONTENTS

·

PREFACE TO THE REISSUE, 1971

THE PRESENT VOLUME, with the exception of the concluding chapter, represents the text of the Haskell Lectures for 1961–1962, delivered to the Graduate School of Theology, Oberlin College, in March 1962. It was a special pleasure for me to return to Oberlin on this occasion, and I wish to record my appreciation of the many kindnesses shown me and Mrs. Wilder by Dean Roger Hazelton, Professor Thomas S. Kepler, and other members of the Faculty of the School. I also wish to acknowledge the generous provision for secretarial assistance provided by the Harvard Divinity School and the skillful preparation of the typescript by various members of the staff, especially Mrs. Arthur Kooman and Mrs. James M. H. Gregg. The Scripture quotations in this publication are unless otherwise indicated from the Revised Standard Version of the Bible, copyrighted 1946 and 1952 by the Division of Christian Education of the National Council of the Churches of Christ in the U.S.A., and used by permission. Grateful acknowledgement is made also to the following publishers for permission to quote from the works cited: to Harcourt, Brace, Jovanovich, Inc., New York, and Faber & Faber, Ltd, London, for four lines from 'Little Gidding' by T. S. Eliot, from *Four Quartets;* to Random House, Inc., the William Morris Agency, and Eyre & Spottiswoode Ltd, for five lines from 'The Child Next Door' by Robert Penn Warren, from *Promises: Poems 1954–1956,* © copyright 1955 and 1957 by Robert Penn Warren.

A.N.W.

INTRODUCTION TO THE REISSUE, 1971

THIS REISSUE OFFERS me an opportunity in this Introduction to locate more particularly the aim and method of the work, to discuss the significance of this approach in current biblical interpretation, and to take account of some of the most recent developments in the specifically 'literary' and rhetorical aspects of New Testament study.

At the outset I would like to indicate in summary fashion three areas in which I try to gather up older pursuits and achievements and carry them farther.

1. Where familiar expositions of the Bible as literature, largely in terms of the Authorized Version, have in the past operated with now dated canons of appreciation and with inappropriate categories of style and genre, I have sought here to deal directly with the original texts and in the light both of contemporary New Testament scholarship and of contemporary 'secular' literary method.

2. Where New Testament scholarship has indeed made major advances in what is known as 'form-criticism'—the identification of various literary and pre-literary or oral elements in the writings with their special features of style: language-patterns eloquent of the particular situation of their origin and rehearsal—I have sought here to combine these insights with others afforded by a contemporary literary criticism and our newer exploration of language and hermeneutic.

3. With respect to the aesthetic aspects of religious language whether as genre or as symbol, whether metaphor or mythos, I have sought to overcome the limitations of much unimaginative interpretation of the New Testament, limitations associated either with a conventional theological approach, or with academic formalism.

I

As a background for this whole undertaking I find it illuminating to recall an older approach to the literary study of the Scriptures under the heading 'The Bible as literature'. The motives and literary criteria of the writers in question are highly revealing with respect to the terms of my present task. In their own setting these authors also wished rightly to bring the Scriptures into some more persuasive relation to general literature. When we read them today we can see what changes have overtaken both the aesthetic and the theology presupposed. In that context the literary aspects of the Bible had to be rigidly set apart from the dogmatic, so much so that the treatments often have an unreal and artificial character. Today with the deepening of all our categories we shall still wish to distinguish art and religion, but we can recognize a much greater common ground and reciprocity in all the uses of language.

On its side comparative literature as a critical discipline has been slow to include biblical texts in its material. It is difficult to include the canonical writings in the humanistic category of literature, especially when their status as Holy Writ has had such a crucial and authoritative role in the life of the West. If the believer assigns his Scriptures to a status *sui generis* it is not surprising that the literary critic finds himself brought to a pass at this fence. It is not as though all religious texts are so treated. Comparative literature can give attention to the holy books of India or to the Gilgamesh Epic. They can be brought into such general genres as saga, folklore, or epic. But our western holy books have still resisted such assimilation, especially the New Testament.

The impediment lies not only in their character as Scripture. It is traceable also to a long history in which biblical scholarship has had its own special methods and tradition. Even today when the biblical writings can more easily be viewed apart from their dogmatic status, the habits of humanistic scholarship and philology constitute a formidable obstacle to their inclusion in the agenda of comparative literature. One deeper factor here is the long orientation of rhetorical and literary studies to Hellenic and humanist criteria. Another factor, no doubt, is the limited place of Semitic studies in our universities since the Renaissance.

Nevertheless one can point to some initiatives in this area. Matthew Arnold concerned himself with the biblical literature in an effort to liberate it from those dogmatic overlays which in his eyes obscured its universal import, overlays which he called *Aberglaube* or superstition or theosophy. He was thus able to include the Scriptures in general literature by de-canonizing them, or by secularizing them as we would say today. But his criteria for literature such as 'power' or 'high poetical quality', which opposed the emotional 'idea' to the fact, exhibited a split of sensibility which could not do justice either to the nature of language itself or to the language of Scripture.[1] The inadequacy of his criteria is confirmed by his conclusion that 'sweet reasonableness' was the dominant note of Jesus' teaching.

How unexpected it was for the humanist to turn to the Bible for literary-critical purposes is well illustrated by Gilbert Murray in *The Rise of the Greek Epic*.[2] In discussing the antecedents of Homer and the history of oral tradition he writes: 'The best parallel for our present purposes is, I think, that of the Hebrew Scriptures. I often wonder that the comparison has not been more widely used by Greek scholars'.[3] He then summarizes the familiar analysis of the sources of the Pentateuch into J, E, D, and P. But his dated aesthetic appears (and one which offers too easy a basis for comparison) as he reaches the climax of his praise of Homer. 'Intensity of imagination is the important thing', he exclaims. And he illustrates this norm by Homer's description of the beauty and tears of Helen, paralleled with that of the account in II Kings 9.20 of the chariot driving of Jehu as reported by the watchman: 'the driving is like the driving of Jehu the son of Nimshi for he driveth furiously'.

> We knew nothing about the driving of Jehu before. We hear no word more about it afterwards. But the one sentence has behind it just that intensity of imagination which makes thoughts live and vibrate like new things a hundred, or a thousand, or two thousand, years after their first utterance. And that is the quality that one finds in Homer.[4]

A new and more discriminating break-through in the literary study of both Testaments came much later in the first two chapters

---

[1] See Ian Gregor, 'Literary Criticism and Religious Belief: A Text and Two Responses', Draft Paper #1 for the Conference on Method in the Study of Literature and Theology, Boston College, September 1969. See also Helen Gardner, *The Business of Criticism* (Oxford 1959), pp. 84–86.

[2] Oxford 1907.

[3] *Ibid.*, 101.

[4] *Ibid.*, 223.

of Erich Auerbach's *Mimesis* (1953), with his examination of biblical and classical styles. We thus leap ahead of our story only to suggest the contrast between an impressionistic criticism and one informed by a more perceptive view both of man and of language.

The writing of books on 'the Bible as literature' which goes back to the beginning of this century was motivated by concerns like those of Matthew Arnold. These authors sought to confine themselves to literary appreciation and to the 'human nature' evoked in the Bible and thus to avoid or go behind dogmatic and theological considerations. There was a laudable intention here to overcome the isolation of the Scriptures from their place in world literature and to open up their intrinsic appeal to 'the common reader' (to cite the title of Mary Ellen Chase's well-known work).[5] It was rightly recognized that most of the exposition of the Bible for the laity at the time—whether for religious education in the churches or for college courses—was shaped to the ends of devotion and edification or dominated by the concerns of biblical criticism. Authors like Richard G. Moulton,[6] of the University of Chicago, J. H. Gardiner of Harvard,[7] Charles A. Dinsmore[8] and William Lyon Phelps[9] both of Yale, and Miss Chase of Smith College; all, with the exception of Dinsmore, professors of English literature, sought to extend to the Bible the modes of analysis and appreciation current in the general study of literature.

In the American scene a special factor was the problem of biblical instruction in the non-sectarian college. Before the establishment of departments of religion, and even later, courses in the biblical literature were taught in the English department, and non-dogmatic texts were in demand. The instructors wrestled with the problem of combining an appreciation of the King James Bible and its influence with some initiation of the student into the complexities of biblical criticism. Older alumni often reminisce about these classes as either snap courses or as among those that were unforgetable. At Harvard there has been a long tradition of such courses taught in the English department. At one time in the twenties there was a lacuna, and the great New Testament scholars

---

[5] *The Bible and the Common Reader* (New York 1944).
[6] *The Literary Study of the Bible: An Account of the Leading Forms of Literature Represented in the Sacred Writings* (Boston 1895).
[7] *The Bible as English Literature* (New York 1906)
[8] *The English Bible as Literature* (Boston and New York 1931).
[9] *Reading the Bible* (New York 1919).

Kirsopp Lake and James Hardy Ropes were prevailed upon to accept the novel task, Lake choosing the Old Testament because, he alleged, he knew little or nothing about it. In this connection it should be said that in this period there were biblical scholars in the seminaries and the universities who brought a high literary sensitivity to their philology. A striking example of this is Robert H. Pfeiffer's *Introduction to the Old Testament*, though again we can today recognize in it the older canons of aesthetic appreciation.

Illustrative of the older procedures is the compilation edited by R. G. Moulton and others, *The Bible as Literature*, published in 1896. Moulton, who taught both at Chicago and in Cambridge University, was best known for his *Modern Reader's Bible: Presented in Modern Literary Form* (1895), which by its typographical arrangements of the material and its eloquent introductions reached a very large public. The contributors to the compilation in question were J. F. Genung, the well-known professor of rhetoric at Amherst; Albert Stanborough Cook, for many years editor of the Yale Studies in English; Henry Van Dyke; and many biblical scholars and theologians.

Lyman Abbott begins his Introduction to the book as follows: 'There are two ways in which we may approach the Bible: the theological and the literary'. By 'literary' he means both humane literary appreciation and historical criticism. Objections to this proper approach he traces in part to 'Puritan intellectual habits. The Puritan was essentially prosaic. He looked with suspicion on the great poet who belonged to his own school,—Milton,—and he condemned unsparingly the still greater poet who did not,—Shakespeare'.[10]

In this Introduction as elsewhere in the book we find the diversity of Scripture identified anachronistically with modern genres: Esther is an 'historical romance', Ruth an 'idyll', Job an 'epic of the inner life', and the books of the prophets are 'volumes of sermons'. The wisdom books are 'philosophy' and the discourses of Moses 'orations'. One must sympathize with the impulse of these liberal interpreters not to let the Bible be 'smothered by Reverence'. The aim was to exalt it as 'literature of power', to be 'read like any other book'. But tell-tale romantic clichés distress us. We read of 'epic gems'. Genesis is, for children, 'the most charming book in the Bible'. We recognize a romantic aesthetic, one closely associated

[10] *The Modern Reader's Bible: Presented in Modern Literary Form* (New York 1895), p. xiii.

with philosophical idealism. But the biblical religion itself was by the same token construed in terms of the simple contrast of a lower and a higher level of reality, the natural and the spiritual. The natural was not disparaged but the order of sense had to be transfigured.

It becomes evident that these interpreters of the Bible as literature thought of the Kingdom of God as a domain of spiritual sensibility, of Beauty, Truth, and Goodness. The discussion of the parables of Jesus tends to a cloudy spirituality. 'The parables, therefore, by means of the facts in the world of sense, picture great corresponding truths in the spiritual world'.[11] But this reigning Zeitgeist, as in the case of Renan's *Life of Jesus*, scanted the heart of the matter. More significantly for our present purposes it could not identify correctly the *literary* features of the Bible. Even at this rhetorical level more justice could have been done if not to the theological import of the writings at least to the peculiar presuppositions and outlook of older epochs. Fortunately at the very time that these essays were being written, justice was beginning to be done to the biblical literary forms by such scholars as Hermann Gunkel, Eduard Norden, Franz Overbeck, and Paul Wendland.

Mary Ellen Chase's *Bible and the Common Reader*, published as late as 1944, is interesting in this context. Writing as a teacher of English literature she observes, 'I have enjoyed no literary adventures as I have enjoyed those within the pages of the Old and New Testaments.' She wishes to communicate her own enthusiasm, especially for the Authorized Version, as well as to overcome such deplorable ignorance as that of one of her students who informed her that Elijah was the heroine of *Uncle Tom's Cabin*. As she observed elsewhere her experience in the war years had reinforced her conviction that 'we should look upon the Bible literally as the cornerstone of our country'. Insisting on the importance of historical backgrounds, she is instructed in the current views of Hebrew literary types. Writing for a popular audience she understandably does not elaborate on certain more fundamental questions as to the rhetoric. But we are still confronted with too confident a view of what the terms 'literary' or 'artistic' connote in contrast with 'religious' or 'theological'. This appears especially in connection with Part III on the New Testament.

[11] Page 239.

The purpose of the New Testament is overwhelmingly religious, and its literary excellence arises almost entirely from the religious fervour of its authors; the Old Testament is a work of literature as well as one of religion, and as literature it is vastly superior to the New.[12]

The men who wrote the New Testament were not men of great literary genius like many of those who wrote the Old . . . They may not have been able to lend to their compositions the artistic distinction of the most memorable books and passages of the Old Testament; but they were able to place upon their rolls of papyrus an undying ardor which has made their literature peculiarly beautiful and their messages to mankind immortal.[13]

One can appreciate what Miss Chase means here, and many others have felt this way. But passages like this exhibit the dilemma of the very category of the Bible 'as literature'. How far is our understanding of the literary, the artistic, the beautiful to be determined by the sensibility of a period or even an epoch? What view of man, of humanism, of reality is determinative? If the aesthetic and the other-than-aesthetic are to be fundamentally distinguished, how and where does one apply the scalpel in separating one from the other in such writings as those of the Bible? There will always remain some unanswered questions in these operations. We cannot but flinch when such terms as 'genius' and 'masterpiece' are invoked, such attributes as 'charm' and 'studied art'.

One cannot but sympathize with the predicament in which college teachers of the Bible as literature found themselves in this period. They wished to commend the Scriptures and the Authorized Version in an academic context where dogmatic aspects were tabu. The wide-ranging scope of such instruction is well suggested in the compilation edited by another Smith College teacher, Margaret B. Crook, *The Bible and Its Literary Associations*.[14] In this book formal features of the Scriptures are treated with attention to comparative literature and folklore.[15] Here the book by the Semitic and Arabic scholar, Duncan Black MacDonald, *The Hebrew Literary Genius*,[16] represented a notable contribution. This author appeals back beyond the stifling mountains of biblical criticism and its frag-

[12] *Ibid.* . p. 262.
[13] *Ibid.*, p. 263–264.
[14] New York 1937.
[15] See also Laura H. Wild, *A Literary Guide to the Bible: A Study of the Types of Literature Present in the Old and New Testaments* (New York 1922, 1928).
[16] Princeton 1933.

mentation of Scripture to the great pioneer works on the national literature of Israel by Bishop Lowth (1710–1787) and Herder (1744–1803), and frankly allies himself with this Romantic tradition. Lowth, the classicist, in his *De Sacra Poesi Hebraeorum* imposed the categories of the Greek and Latin classics, but 'his study was a study in pure literature'. Herder, writing at a time when many primitive literatures had become accessible, was also able to regard the Old Testament as part of the literary expression of the human race. MacDonald himself brings a rich expertise in the humanism of the ancient Near East to bear upon the language, rhetoric, and wisdom of Israel, though still in that Romantic tradition.

Though in this book we confine our attention to the New Testament, we cannot but take into account the original focus of Lowth and Herder on the unique creativeness and morphology of the literature of Israel as a people. While the Romantic presuppositions of their insights have had their sequel in more recent forms of sentimentality—in consequence of the progressive dissociation of sensibility in our culture—yet their work brought the biblical writings into the total conspectus of world literature. In this sense we are their debtors. Yet as literary students we are still left with the problem of the specifically religious and revelational aspects of this literature, even if one can distinguish between the writings themselves and the sacred character assigned them canonically by Judaism and Christianity. At this point we should frankly recognize that the gap between the literary and the confessional approach cannot be closed. Though, from the point of view of anthropology and psychology, religion and art may appear to be consubstantial in their genesis, yet plain-speaking Samuel Johnson can hardly be controverted: 'Contemplative piety, or the intercourse between God and the human soul, cannot be poetical. Man, admitted to implore the mercy of his Creator, and plead the merits of the Redeemer, is already in a higher state than poetry can confer'.[17]

If then, we should hold all such ultimate questions open, yet both the study of secular literature and that of the Bible or of any 'holy books' can be mutually illuminating and, in all penultimate matters, can be brought within the same purview. Here at least we can see the flagrant artificiality of the older approach to the Bible as

---

[17] *Life of Waller*, cited by E. E. Phare, *The Poetry of Gerard Manley Hopkins* (Cambridge 933), pp. 106–107.

*older
younger*

literature. Its declared hiatus between the literary approach and
the theological obscured common elements and put much properly
literary observation out of court. It was based not on an intrinsic
demarcation but upon a culturally determined academic and
aesthetic dogma associated with Victorian sensibility. Today we
have moved beyond either an idealist aesthetic in art or a theological rationalism in religion, and wide common ground is
opened up in our total exploration of language and its uses.

It comes, then, with some surprise to find a new book with the
old title, *The Bible as Literature*, published in 1970, and written by
a Cambridge University scholar, T. R. Henn.[18] One turns to it
with some incredulity to see how the author conceives his undertaking. He recognizes in his first words that the title 'is clearly
open to many and grave objections. The first task, therefore, is to
attempt to strip it of pejorative or superficial associations, and
suggest some kind of redefinition and method of control'. One
objection to the title is that any such vast miscellany cannot have
the unity appropriate to a work of literature. Its unity is 'spiritual'
and that falls outside 'the terms of this essay'. Yet how far, then,
'can the Bible be considered as literature, in any coherent sense?'
One reply is that it 'has been burned deeply into the fabric of the
life and literature of the English-speaking peoples'. The author, we
see, has already turned to the English translations, and he elects
the Authorized Version. But he also recognizes that as literature
the Scripture must be broken down 'into arbitrarily-chosen
examples of the "kinds", such as epic, narrative, lyric, dramatic,'
and that he must offer 'some consideration of them by means of the
normal critical methods'.

But then, again, the real question is raised: 'the phrase "the
Bible as literature" suggests, perhaps, a method of approach . . .
which is in some way spurious'. And he quotes C. S. Lewis:

> It may be asked whether now, when only a minority of Englishmen
> regard the Bible as a sacred book, we may anticipate an increase of its
> literary influence. I think we might if it continued to be widely read.
> But this is not very likely. Our age has indeed coined the expression
> 'the Bible as literature'. It is very generally implied that those who have
> rejected its theological pretensions nevertheless continue to enjoy it as
> a treasure-house of English prose. It may be so. There may be people
> who, having been forced upon familiarity with it by believing parents,

[18] New York 1970.

have yet been drawn to it by its literary charms and remained as
constant readers. But I never happen to meet them.[19]

The nub of the objection by C. S. Lewis appears when he remarks
that 'The Bible is so remorselessly and continuously sacred that it
does not invite, it excludes or repels, the merely aesthetic approach'.[20]

Henn demurs at some points. He notes the rising circulation of
the Bible in many languages and versions. He is aware that the
literary approach may be charged with something like dilettantism
and may give offence whether by insisting on the unity of form and
content in the texts, or on a more faithful translation of dubious
passages, or by a refusal of archaic interpretations and hidden
meanings. Yet the author goes some length to defend figurative
interpretation and enrichments of the sense which are 'the product
of ancient wisdom and meditation'. He rejects verbal inspiration.
He also rejects 'the modern trend of the "demythologizing"
theologians', as well as the 'loose superlatives and generalizations
that so often attend the writings . . . of those who have taken as their
title, "The Bible as Literature"'. How he proposes to redefine the
task is best suggested by the following: 'a study such as this . . .
must attempt to draw into itself a range of literary comparisons and
exempla that is wider than many might think proper. In justification
I would suggest that this aspect of the importance of the Bible can
best be shown by some alignment with aspects of secular literature,
and with art and iconography'. His deeper presupposition as to the
border line of 'literature' and Scripture is suggested by a rather
unexpected appeal to archetypes and 'mythologems' in the
biblical records which, by the help of the creative imagination,
satisfy the deepest need of the psyche and nourish the life of the
spirit.

This book by Henn does move beyond the older approaches to
the Bible as literature. As a literary scholar, an authority on Yeats
and the Irish poets in particular, the author brings a rich gamut
of sophisticated inquiry to bear upon Scripture. He is at his best
in showing how 'the normal methods of literary study' can dis-
burden the Bible reader of gratuitous obstacles associated with so
ancient a library. He is particularly effective in his validation of

[19] Quoted from C. S. Lewis, *They Asked for a Paper:* The Literary Influence of the
Authorized Version (London 1962).
[20] *Ibid.*

what seem the exotic imagery, fable, and folk-lore of so alien a literature.

The critical issue arises here again, however, as to how he sees the line between 'literature' and revelation. The decision on this matter inevitably affects a writer's view of the particular rhetorics of the Bible. At this point Henn is to be placed in the older tradition of those who have written on the Bible as literature. It is true that he would dissociate himself from an older aesthetic. Thus he is dissatisfied with 'such terms as "sublime", "majestic", "noble", "exalting", which can be traced back to "Longinus" and in particular, to his re-interpretation at the hands of the eighteenth-century critics. Much Victorian criticism of the Bible employs these terms: which assume our ability to respond to "great thoughts" expressed in "an eminence and excellence of language'.[21]

Yet Henn, assenting with some qualifications to C. S. Lewis' proposition that the Bible is 'remorselessly and continuously sacred', leaves an unnecessarily wide gulf between the literary and the religious approach. He comes closest to bridging these in what he says about archetypes and the spirit, as noted above, and most clearly in his closing paragraphs where he notes how 'as the literary approach exhausts itself we begin to perceive the infinite'. Here he cites at length from Wordsworth's *Prelude* on the power of the Imagination. But this kind of transcendentalism leaves too many questions unanswered.

It is not our view that this gap can be altogether closed. But there are newer approaches to rhetoric and language in their relation to reality which are not employed in Henn's work. These insights apply to any human utterance, sacred or secular. They have, in fact, become mandatory in dealing with much of contemporary literature in which the mutations of genre as well as the revolution in sensibility elude the control of older categories. These strategies have been abundantly fruitful in dealing with the language and styles of the New Testament. But they also deepen our grasp of the literary arts.

II

Our review of the 'Bible as literature' approach may serve as a foil to the new contributions made possible today by a wide range

[21] *Ibid.*, p. 248, n. 1.

of procedures and perspectives associated with a contemporary literary criticism. Granted that a prior concern still obtains to bring the biblical writings into the purview of general literature, yet this should be done in such a way as to safeguard and even enhance their distinctiveness. This was not possible in a period dominated by an aesthetic idealism which, moreover, obscured the proper understanding of secular literature itself. The advantages of the present situation lie first of all in our post-Romantic grasp of all rhetorics, but then also in the availability of the more recent tools of criticism. What furthers the reassessment is the fact that in biblical criticism also the same changing horizon of interpretation has had its effect and that some of the same procedures have born notable fruit.

It is truly a matter of some astonishment that the term 'literary criticism' should have such different connotations for biblical scholars as for students of literature generally. It is true that any assessment of ancient texts involves the critic to a special degree in questions of provenance, authorship, sources, dating, and purpose. But biblical 'literary criticism' has generally confined itself to such questions. Those appreciative and interpretive operations which are the goal of criticism everywhere else, also with respect to the classics, have until recently been assigned to exegesis and biblical theology, apart from some special areas of observation such as the identification of Hebrew metrics. This restricted sense of biblical criticism has become so fixed that the study of properly literary features has had to be carried out in separate disciplines such as *Gattungskritik* and form-criticism, or special areas like comparative saga and mythology.

But the situation is changing today. There is a new appreciation of the inseparable relation of form and content in all texts as well as of the individual writings viewed as literary wholes or aesthetic objects in terms of their overall structure. This new approach so familiar in secular letters can be combined with wider investigations today of language in all its modes, both with respect to genres and to symbolics. It is not therefore surprising that the cleavage between literary and biblical criticism is being narrowed.

For a discussion of some of the factors that have been operating in these recent changes, whether in literary or biblical criticism or in their interaction, we can turn to two recent writers, one a New Testament scholar and the other a literary critic.

In his recent book, *Literary Criticism of the New Testament*,[22] William A. Beardslee at the outset considers the factors which justify the wider scope of his treatment. Of particular interest is his observation that one main line of tradition of literary criticism, a line that has largely dominated the literary study of the New Testament, traces to Aristotle's *Rhetoric* rather than to his *Poetics*. This tradition

> treats the form as vehicle for a content which can stand in its own right, apart from the form. Form, from this point of view, becomes simply a means for effectively (persuasively) communicating the content, which in turn is thought of as an idea. Since persuasion was the aim of ancient rhetoric, and since persuasion has also been an important aim not only for the New Testament writers but for those who have studied them in later times, it is not surprising that many of the approaches to literary study of the New Testament should have been in terms of this type of analysis . . . This line of thinking fits in well with the heavily theological tradition of Christianity.[23]

Beardslee recognizes that the thematic interpretation of the New Testament writings has had its rights, but the total understanding of the writings has been prejudiced by the rhetorical starting point. It has also been obscured, he notes, by 'the sharply historical cast of so much biblical scholarship'. The quest for secure foundations for the faith has motivated the inquiry into deeper strata of the tradition, for the earliest sources and for original historical data— all of which has drawn attention away from the writings as they stand. In the process valuable findings have been made with respect to older rhetorical patterns, liturgical, gnomic, narrative, and so forth, but all such literary excavation needed to be supplemented by a more total approach.

Here Beardslee invokes the second line of tradition of literary criticism descended from Aristotle's *Poetics*, one which links form, content, and function in the literary work, and one which has proved so fruitful in recent criticism. But the critics have confined the use of this model largely to 'self-conscious literary works' and have supposed that such writings as those of the New Testament were not amenable to the same strategies. It is true that the

[22] Philadelphia 1970. It is worth noting that this title is one of a series devoted to biblical scholarship of the New Testament all 'literary', the other two titles being: 'What is Form Criticism?' and 'What is Redaction Criticism?' All three aspects are interrelated.

[23] *Ibid.*, p. 3–4.

particular tests and morphologies that have furthered general criticism in this tradition are ill-suited to the writings of the canon. But when these writings are located in the wider context of folk literature and popular literature, the model of the *Poetics* can be adapted with significant results.

Beardslee's appeal to Aristotelian models relates importantly to the scholarly discipline of New Testament studies. The tradition of the *Rhetoric* has encouraged a thematic reading of the texts which the theological concerns of the Church understandably furthered. For this or similar reasons even the Song of Songs had been made to teach a lesson, and the theology of the Book of Revelation was set side by side with that of Paul's epistles.

In the more popularized treatments of Scripture represented by books on the 'Bible as literature' the particular aesthetic that came to our attention was the Romantic or the idealist. Though these writers were in revolt against a theological interpretation, their approach can also be assigned to the tradition of the *Rhetoric*. For them, the eloquent or the naive, the vivid or the sublime—yes, the purple passages—were highlighted; all those decorative or ingratiating or quasi-magical features which a writer or orator marshals to effect persuasion. But here too we recognize a model which draws attention away from the unity of the work.

On this whole matter of changing method we turn to observations from quite a different quarter. Helen Gardner, writing on 'The Limits of Literary Criticism',[24] provides us with a delightful instance of the literary scholar looking over the fence at what is going on in New Testament study. Between New Testament criticism and Shakespeare criticism she writes,

> there are connections, some arising from the intellectual habits of the age, some due to cross-fertilization. As a professional student of secular literature, I tend to feel when I read certain recent works in New Testament criticism that I am finding familiar tools taken up and used on unfamiliar materials.[25]

While this author is mainly concerned with 'modern methods of literary criticism and the problems they raise', she cannot but recognize that such discussion 'has an obvious bearing on a matter which is of great importance to Christians, the interpretation of Holy Scripture'.

[24] Part II of *The Business of Criticism* (Oxford 1959).
[25] *Ibid.*, p. 80.

What specially interests us here is the correlation she notes between certain successive phases of study in the two areas. Fixing her attention on the period after Matthew Arnold and Benjamin Jowett—concerned as they were with moral sentiment and the religious or human universal—she observes in biblical criticism the increasingly exhaustive analysis of the writings and their sources and the identification of borrowed motifs and myths. This fragmentation of the texts had its counterpart in literary studies of the time. To redress the situation she then notes a new concern with the writings as wholes—the work as it stands in its relative autonomy. At this point Miss Gardner evidently touches upon one of the most significant features of recent biblical study as well as of general criticism.

In literary criticism attention has now for some time been directed to the given work as a self-sufficient aesthetic whole which should be allowed to make its own impact apart from extraneous considerations having to do with the author and his circumstances or intentions or with distinctions between matter and form. The particular 'word' of the poem, play, or novel is to be encountered at the level of its own coherent and interrelated pattern of imagery and design. Such a plea for the properly autonomous creation of the artist represents a persuasive protest against that kind of criticism which obscures the unity of the work either by pre-occupation with isolated elements or by some didactic concern. We note here also an insistence on the particularity of the imaginative act as against all romanticizing views which in effect neglect the formal and concrete aspect of art and language in favor of a looser inspirational rhetoric. Especially in the study of the gospels in the last two decades we have seen a corresponding major development in New Testament studies. Literary assessment has moved from the analysis of the formal elements appropriated by the evangelists to a recognition of the total structure of each gospel.

Miss Gardner addresses herself to this stage of literary criticism both in secular letters and in biblical study. Her title, 'The Limits of Criticism', reflects her concern with certain abuses in this approach. She is particularly critical of the lengths to which some Elizabethan scholars have gone in exploiting image-analysis. The meaning of a poem or a play is not disclosed if we attend only to the symbolic patterns that the author weaves. It is not enough to identify some such dominant and interrelated imaginative structure as though it existed outside of time and place. Such an approach to meaning through form and pattern is blind, for example, to the notion that meaning also inheres in style which, by contrast, is a very personal thing.

This particular abuse of literary criticism had had its older analogies in New Testament criticism in certain forms of allegorical interpretation. At the present stage it does not seem to be a pressing danger. But Miss Gardner does find a contemporary example in Austin Farrer's studies in the Gospel of Mark.[26] This scholar seeks to restore to us the impact of this Gospel as a total imaginative experience. He identifies in the work an elaborate and self-consistent architecture of symbolic correspondences related also to Old Testament antecedents. It is in this sense that he speaks of the 'poetry of St. Mark', not meaning merely its artistry, and not with the intention of contrasting 'poetry' with 'history'. His impulse to validate the gospel-form in its total pattern is unobjectionable as is his appreciation of the dynamic significance of early Christian symbolics. One can remain unpersuaded as to the cogency of the elaborate symbolic structures he identifies just as a critic can demur at many points with respect to the literary-historical judgments of the author about the gospel-tradition and Mark's use of it. But beyond that, as Miss Gardner observes, it is not enough in the case of such a work to know how the imagination of an author works. For the import of the work we should be able to recognize the intention of the writer as distinct from the symbolic patterns he weaves, especially since these patterns belong to a distant past. The author 'was a man, not a disembodied imagination. He was writing a work in which his readers would find things able to make them wise unto salvation'.[27] In other words, granted that a work should be read as an interrelated whole, we encounter it not only as an art-work of the imagination but as a voice that goes on speaking in many modalities not only to the imagination but to all aspects of our apprehension including reason and will.

If, then, a main contribution of secular literary criticism to New Testament study bears on the wholeness of the writing or unit, whether gospel or apocalypse or parable, this approach nevertheless needs to be scrutinized. Miss Gardner's discussion offers one example of such scrutiny. In reacting against older selective ways of

[26] *A Study in St. Mark* (London 1951); *St. Matthew and St. Mark* (London 1954).
[27] *Ibid.*, p. 122.

finding relevant meaning in a play or a poem—or in a biblical form
—one can go too far in a contrary direction. Instead of isolating
particular elements in a work at the expense of its total impact, one
can isolate the work as a whole, defined by its self-sufficient aesthetic
pattern, from any wider world of meaning. Objections of this kind
against the 'new criticism' have become familiar among literary
critics.

A further example of such objection at a deeper level is found in
what is known as existential criticism, and here our reading both
of general letters and of New Testament texts is clearly at stake.
This approach as directed to the interpretation of general literature
parts company with the 'new criticism' as commonly practised.
'Meaning' is related not to the literary work as object, even when
taken as a whole, but to that ultimate Real or Being itself which
discloses itself in the work, in the language event of which the work
is only the vehicle. Here the theologian recognizes the categories of
interpretation made familiar by Bultmann's followers in the 'new
hermeneutic'. But these same categories are now being invoked for
literary and aesthetic criticism.

Of particular importance here is the book by Hans-Georg
Gadamer, *Wahrheit und Methode*,[28] which builds on Heidegger to
present a general hermeneutic not only for the arts and humanities
but for all human acts of understanding and language. The
categories and theses of this study correspond at many points with
those of contemporary theologians concerned with language, and
especially with those New Testament interpreters identified with
the 'new heremeneutic'. Here we can mention specially the work
of James M. Robinson and the symposium, *The New Hermeneutic*,[29]
for which he supplied the lengthy and perceptive introduction. The
use of this approach in the literary study of the New Testament
forms has proved particularly fruitful in the work of Robert W.
Funk, notably in his *Language, Hermeneutic, and the Word of God*,[30]
but also in more limited studies such as that by Don A. Via, Jr.,
The Parables: Their Literary and Existential Dimensions,[31] not to
mention the work of German scholars like Ernst Fuchs and
Gerhard Ebeling.

---

[28] Tübingen 1960.
[29] Edited by J. M. Robinson and J. B. Cobb, Jr. (New York 1964).
[30] New York 1966.
[31] Philadelphia 1967.

The reciprocity of theological and humanistic labors in this field, as well as of American and European workers,[32] has been strikingly manifest in the series of Consultations on hermeneutics at Drew University in the sixties, culminating in 1966 when students of literature like Kenneth Burke, Julian Morías and Owen Barfield participated. The discussions, published under the title, *Interpretation: The Poetry of Meaning*,[33] related various types of existential method to other approaches to language and meaning. It is important to recognize that our better understanding today of the dynamics of human speech and writing and of their symbolic structures requires that we confront the line represented by Bultmann—Heidegger—Gadamer with all that we can learn from social-psychology and from French phenomenologists like Paul Ricoeur. Here the book by Ray L. Hart, *Unfinished Man and the Imagination*,[34] represents an invaluable synthesis.

To return to existential criticism itself, we may cite the book of Richard E. Palmer, *Hermeneutics: Interpretive Theory in Schleiermacher, Dilthey, Heidegger, and Gadamer*.[35] This author rejects the approach of the new critics. He does not wish to return to an older idealist aesthetic or to deny the unity of a literary text. But he sees these critics as still prisoners of an old subject-object mentality long associated with our whole western view of reality. In this context the play or the poem is an object to be mastered or delighted in. But

> to start with considerations of form means that even at the outset literary interpretation has fallen away from the unity and fulness of the aesthetic moment.
>
> The beginning point for literary interpretation must be the language event of experiencing the work itself—i.e., what the work 'says'. The saying power of a literary work, not its form, is the ground of our meaningful encounter with it, and is not something separate from the form but rather speaks in and through the form . . . The saying done by a literary work is a disclosure of being; its shining forth is the power of the truth of being . . . Language has the power to say, to bring a world to stand. That is what Heidegger means when he says, with Hölderlin, that man dwells 'poetically' on this earth.[36]

---

[32] See Hermann Mörchen, *Rilkes Sonette an Orpheus* (Stuttgart 1958). This extensive study of Rilke is written by a literary critic associated with the Bultmann circle ("Die alte Marburger") and its method.

[33] Edited by Stanley R. Hopper and David L. Miller (New York 1967).

[34] New York 1968.

[35] Evanston 1969.

[36] *Ibid.*, p. 248.

This emphasis on meaning in the work of art as existentially appropriated corresponds to that of the 'new hermeneutic'. In both cases we have to do with a language event which transcends the subject-object relation so that what is said stands disclosed in a way that unites text and reader, past and present. In the following chapters this view of language is accepted. But only with reservations. We recognize the claustrophobic error of treating a writing as an autonomous aesthetic object. We agree that meaning emerges in our reciprocal encounter with the work. But we are dissatisfied with the vague generality of such terms as the 'unveiling' or 'unconcealment' of Being to characterize such meaning. Granted that some forms of modern subjectivity are in this way overcome, we seem nevertheless to be driven in the conditions of our own Zeitgeist to resolve all complexities by some too easy formula for ultimacy. In theological hermeneutics this takes the form of a leap through the various particular 'language events' of the sacred texts to the Word of God in its immediacy. But here the rich and various structures of religious experience are short-changed as appears, for example, in the impulse to a premature demythologizing of the symbolic elements. In philosophy and aesthetics as well as in the post-modern sensibility as a whole it takes the form often of a quest for Being in its purity or some immaculate Word.

Another version of existential criticism in modern letters is that associated with the French and Swiss-French 'critics of consciousness'.[37] These writers also part company with the new criticism. Though not appealing to philosophical existentialism they look behind the given writing to the particular pre-verbal experience and imaginative act of the author.

> Literature is not, in effect, language; nor is it a structure composed of language: 'a literary text is above all a living, conscious reality, a thought that thinks to itself and which, in thinking, becomes thinkable to us—a voice that speaks to itself and which, in so speaking, speaks to us from within'.[38]

In viewing the work of literature as an act and not an object these critics often suggest the category of 'language event' without so naming it. This kind of existentialism seeks to do full justice to the

[37] See Sarah Lawall, *Critics of Consciousness: The Existential Structures of Literature* (Cambridge, Mass. 1968).
[38] *Ibid.*, p. 81, citing Georges Poulet.

particularities of different authors and their own contexts and personal myths. Both kinds, however, illuminate the method with which the rhetoric of the New Testament should be studied.

In the following chapters we recognize the novelty of early Christian discourse and language forms, as well as the trans-historical impulse which prompts such novelty and power, and which continues to operate whenever these texts come to speech in new times. But we are constrained to observe and safeguard the particularity and concreteness of each such text. What is crucial here is that all such manifold particularity in the language and the language events—in the various genres, voices, and images—requires a corresponding rich structure in Reality itself, in Being itself. This aspect of the ultimate mystery,—whether the approach be in aesthetic, philosophical, or theological terms—does not always come into its rights in existential criticism and interpretation.

EARLY CHRISTIAN RHETORIC

I

THE NEW UTTERANCE

Jesus Christ, his son, who is his word proceeding from silence.
IGNATIUS, *Ad Magn.* 8.2

The uninterrupted news that grows out of silence.
RILKE, *Sonnets for Orpheus*

MEN OF OUR time have inevitably had their attention called to the problem of language, and in various aspects. As modern devices make the world smaller and smaller, and throw us ever closer to peoples we had thought of as alien and remote, we find ourselves under the necessity of mastering more foreign tongues. But it is not only a matter of diverse languages. We are now more conscious of the problem of communication itself even in our own language. Familiar words have lost their meaning for many; or the same word means different things to different people. Jargon and clichés usurp the place of discriminating speech in many areas of life. It is not only in the modern arts that we wrestle with the problem of meaning. It is not surprising that philosophy is today occupied above all with language, or that social science interests itself in the rhetoric of propaganda, or the Church with the task of communication. In a situation like ours any use of language that aspires to a wide audience, as with mass-entertainment or advertising, has perforce to sink to a very low common denominator of what is not so much language as elementary stimuli by verbal gags, pictures and rhythms.

No doubt we are going through a period of the death and birth of language, one of the primordial features of human nature and culture. We have to become dumb before we can learn to use names and words faithfully again. It is in modern poetry that one sees this struggle most revealingly. In view of all this it is again not surprising that a main concern of the Christian Church today is that of communication. The preacher, we are told, is like a man speaking into a dead microphone. We hear on all sides about the need for the modernization of the Christian message, translation of the ancient ideas and images, rediscovery of effective media of discourse. It has seemed worth while, therefore, to study the speech-forms and utterance of the Early Church and see what we can learn from it.

We are concerned first of all, therefore, not so much with what the early Christians said as how they said it. Yet this is a false distinction. The two cannot really be separated, but they can be looked at separately. We are interested here in all that has to do with the form and style of the New Testament writings. In this sense we are taking a literary approach. One could call it a study of the literary forms and genres of the Early Church. However, we must deal here not only with the writings as such but with the oral speech that lies behind them. It is not only a question of how the first Christians wrote but how they spoke and talked. It is better, therefore, to call our topic, 'early Christian rhetoric'. It is true that the term 'rhetoric' has unfortunate connotations. But it has the advantage of covering both written and oral discourse.

I

Those who are acquainted with New Testament studies know the importance of what is called form-criticism and form-history in the analysis of the Gospels. We are fortunate in having survivals in the Gospels of what Jesus said and did, or of early reports of what he said and did. Most of such carry-overs and vestiges reach us now in the connected narratives of our Gospels. But these writings break down transparently into a large number of short separate episodes or anecdotes and sayings that came down for a considerable period by oral transmission. These units can again be sorted out according to style and character in the light of comparable oral tradition. There are laws of form in social tradition as there are in geology. As Henry J. Cadbury has observed, to look beneath the surface in one of our Gospels is like digging into an ancient mound: one finds successive strata, and in each of them distinctive and tell-tale objects and artifacts.

In the Old Testament scholars have uncovered various formal patterns of language in the poetry and history and codes, reaching far back into a long pre-literary, that is, oral period. Comparative studies of world-wide saga, epic, folk-lore and ritual-texts have thrown a great deal of light upon the ancient oral elements which are embedded in our written Old Testament library. Similarly with the New Testament. What we find, moreover, is not only a question of the forms themselves, say a parable or a doxology or a poem; it is also a question of their matrix—the workshop, as it were, of the earliest Church in which these forms were transmitted and reshaped. All such findings of technical form-criticism we shall keep in mind.

But we would like to go behind this kind of observation to the question of language itself. How does the whole phenomenon of language, speech, communication, rhetoric present itself in the rise of Christianity? What modes of discourse are specially congenial to the Gospel? What is the special role of oral as against written discourse? What is the theological significance of particular rhetorical patterns used or neglected in the Early Church? What comparisons can be drawn in this area between the language of the Gospels and that of contemporary Judaism or Hellenism, or between earlier and later phases of the New Testament Church itself?

To suggest the promise of these lines of inquiry let us cite an analogy: that of the arts. This is relevant, since we are, indeed, concerned here with the arts of language in the Early Church. Different cultures favour different arts. In one culture the drama will be the most representative art-form and reach a high level of perfection. In another culture it may be painting or music. Even in the same culture, changed circumstances will bring about changed priorities in the arts or in their styles. Similarly with religions; one will favour one art-form and may even proscribe another, as Israel restricted the use of the graphic arts, and as certain modern sects have banned the use of the organ. Of course, all faiths avail themselves of language and the arts of language. But there are immense differences here. And it is not only in *what* they say that religions differ, that is, in their doctrines and myths, but also in *how* they speak, in the particular oral and literary vehicles which they prefer. In one religion, or in one religion at one stage, the oracular mode or incantation may be typical; in another the prose-code, in another the philosophical-mystical hymn. In some modern types of Christianity, the rational proposition has been prominent, in others the pure language of Zion. In any given cult or sect, of course, we usually find a variety of rhetorics, but one or other will predominate.

Certain modes of utterance, moreover, are more primitive or naïve than others; the oracle and the cult-story or myth stand nearer the birth of religion than the code. Yet even at a sophisticated level the believer may return to the fountain-head. So in modern painting the artist returns for revitalization to the a-b-c's of sensibility and perception of the primitives.

To return to the particular arts of language of particular periods. These no doubt are conditioned by the cultural heritage and expectation of the setting. Jesus used the parable partly because it was a current and meaningful genre. Paul used the diatribe style for the same reason, and thus could communicate all the more effectively. But the greater speakers and writers, as in these cases also, create new forms and styles or at least renew the old forms, still in relation to their audience. F. O. Matthiessen has shown how Walt Whitman spoke with a new tongue in his declamatory verse, yet found precedents for it in current speech-forms. Whitman saw himself as contributing to 'the growth of an American English enjoying a distinct identity', and wrote, 'I sometimes think the *Leaves* [i.e. *Leaves of Grass*] is only a language experiment.'[1] But the peculiar form of his verse was shaped by contemporary rhetorics, especially as Matthiessen shows, by the cadences of public oratory and of operatic recitative and aria, both reinforcing his belief that poetry was not something written but uttered.[2] In the case of Emerson, the distinctive essay form was shaped from local cultural roots in the New England sermon and the Lyceum lecture tradition. 'I look,' said he, 'upon the lecture-room as the true church of today, and as the home of a richer eloquence than Faneuil Hall or the Capitol ever knew.'[3] Herman Melville, for his part, found his media and style in dependence on patterns familiar to his public, the English Bible and Shakespeare.

We cite these analogies only to suggest, arguing from the lesser to the greater, that the new speech-modes of Jesus and his followers had deep conditioning-factors in the rhetorics of their time, but also in the cultural crisis that demanded new styles. Therefore any study of the rhetorical forms of the New Testament is not a superficial matter. Form and content cannot long be held apart.

We should stress here one implication of our topic to be kept in mind throughout even when we may seem to have forgotten it. The

[1] *American Renaissance* (New York 1941), p. 517. 'He wanted to devise a wholly new speaking style, far more direct and compelling than any hitherto . . .', p. 557.
[2] *Ibid.*, p. 559.
[3] Cited by Matthiessen, *ibid.*, p. 23.

character of the early Christian speech-forms should have much to say to us with regard to our understanding of Christianity and its communication today. We may well go back to the fountain-head of the Gospel in this respect also. This is not to be taken in a trite sense; for example, that because Jesus used parables we also should use illustrations from life, or because the New Testament has a place for poetry we also should use it. All this is true. But there is rather the question of what kind of story and what kind of poetry. Nor should we feel ourselves enslaved to biblical models whether in statement, image or form. But we can learn much from our observations as to the appropriate strategies and vehicles of Christian speech and then adapt these to our own situation. It is significant, for example, how large a place the dramatic mode has in the faith of the Bible and in its forms of expression, even though we find no theatre-art as we know it in the Bible or among the early believers. The important role of religious drama in our churches today has, nevertheless, very specific justification in biblical theology and in New Testament rhetorical forms.

II

In this first chapter we are concerned with the general pheno-menon of language in the New Testament and especially with its novelty. We could take as our text the promise of prophet and psalmist that in the day of salvation God's people would speak with new tongues and sing a new song, and that the mouth of the dumb would be opened. The first Christians felt that these promises had been fulfilled among them. They were conscious of a new endow-ment of language, both freedom of speech and powers of com-munication. Consider what this means. Any human language repre-sents a special kind of order superimposed upon existence. Genera-tions live in it as a habitat in which they are born and die. Outside it is nescience. The language of a people is its fate. Thus the poets or seers who purify the language of the tribe are truly world-makers, and the 'unacknowledged legislators of the world'. Perhaps one can say that nothing affects the significance of human existence more than the range and resource of our articulation, vocabulary, syntax and discourse.[1] Men awaken to a greater plenitude of being as they operate with more signs and names and media of communication,

[1] 'The line between man and beast—between the highest ape and the lowest savage—is the language line'—Suzanne K. Langer.

and so find themselves more aware of their world and its inter-relationships.

Primitive man testifies in various ways to his sense of the mystery and fatefulness of language. Social psychologists tell us that the birth of language and myth is simultaneous with world-making. The primitive does not first see an object and then give it a name. Rather in naming it he calls it into being. Hence the enormous role in such societies of the oracle, the spell, the curse, the blessing. This potency of speech is carried over into advanced cultures by the poet and liturgist. This sense of the power of language is evidenced by children and is reflected in their games as it is in fairy-tales and folk-lore. It is also manifested all about us not only in poetry and in religious language but also in totalitarian political fervour. Moreover, in all such naïve and potent speech certain recurrent patterns are observable, various grooves in which it falls, shapes in which dynamic communication crystallizes: such as the exclamation, the rhythmic chant, the incantation, oracle, spell, injunction, dialogue, ballad, aphorism.

If the naming of things is equivalent to their being called into being, we find ourselves on the same ground with the Genesis account of the creation. God spoke and it was done. Such is the power of the word. Islam has a tradition, indeed, that if one could stumble upon the right word and speak it, the whole universe would vanish in a moment. The word is sovereign.

There is more than first appears in the Old Testament emphasis upon the creation of man by the word of God. It is one thing to picture a deity as fashioning the world and its creatures with his hands. It is still another to think, as the Greeks did, of the soul as a kind of copy of an eternal mind: this represents a more refined kind of anthropomorphism. But to hold that God created man by a word of command and of address, this is something more. A creature that is *called* into being, called by *name*, along with nature, this creature belongs to a more personal order. In the idea of the creative word not only is reason implicit but mutuality and dialogue. Indeed, man is created in the image of God in the sense that he, too, speaks, names and communicates. The Genesis account tells us that God gave Adam the prerogative of naming the creatures and so in a sense calling them into life.[1] The universe of man and of nature is a vast

---

[1] W. Zimmerli, 'Die Weisung des Alten Testamentes zum Geschäft der Sprache', *Das Problem der Sprache in Theologie und Kirche*, ed. W. Schneemelcher (Berlin 1959), p. 3.

scheme not only of intelligence and order, but of answering voices and communion. This is why the Psalmist can proclaim that the earth is full of the steadfast love of the Lord (33.5).

Though early Israel knew nothing of any 'holy language', yet its utterance took on new features as over against the speech-forms of Canaan.[1] We have a parable of this in the report that 'the Lord used to speak to Moses face to face, as a man speaks with his friend' (Ex. 33.11). The rhetorics of the Old Testament represent the response of men to the address of God, and their form and style are elicited by the self-communication of God.[2] Thus this same thirty-third Psalm calls on men to sing a *new* song to God (v.3). And the sanction for such new speech is familiar in Israel's confessional tradition:

> For the word of the Lord is upright;
> and all his work is done in faithfulness . . .

> By the word of the Lord the heavens were made,
> and all their host by the breath of his mouth . . .

> For he spoke, and it came to be;
> he commanded, and it stood forth. (Vv. 4, 6, 9.)

From all this it follows that the whole compendium of Israel's literature is built upon peculiar rhetorics that find no place in the textbooks of Aristotle or Quintilian.

In the new Testament also the word or voice of God is seen as effective, and as bringing in a new thing. We have the theme of the incarnate word in John, and of the shining of the light out of darkness by the creative word in Paul, and indeed the constant identification of the Good News with the word. As we have noted, the new Israel was aware of an endowment with new tongues, for God had again called his people and all men to a new face-to-face hearing or interview in the Gospel.

The Christian movement was creative in various ways, including the phenomena of human discourse. This impulse brought forth not only new vocabulary and oral patterns but also new literary forms and styles. Even in the area of publication we have learned recently

[1] *Ibid.*, p. 19.
[2] *Ibid.*, with reference to the recital pattern in the Psalter; the prominence of the verbal clause in the Old Testament; the all but total disappearance of the adjective in many contexts; the transformation of the style of saga and myth when they are taken over by Israel, pp. 16–17.

that the Early Church was among the first to exploit new procedures, that is in the use of the book or codex-form rather than the scroll.[1] Down to the present day Christianity in its more vital phases has shown itself creative in the arts and media of language.[2] The mere fact of the translation of the Bible into most of the languages and dialects of the globe is a sign of the speech-vitality of Christianity. And this carries with it a pioneer role in linguistics. As has been said:

> No other literary work has been translated into as many languages spoken in as varied a range of cultures as has the Bible. Therefore Bible translators lay claim to a wealth of linguistic data that does not exist elsewhere.

But Christianity has also always been creative in the arts of printing. Recently we have seen the first large-scale use of the computer for literary purposes in the indexing of the Revised Standard Bible. The Church today should be equally prompt in exploiting the new techniques of those mass-media identified with language and publication, especially the radio and recordings. All this is in keeping with the fact that Christianity is a religion of the word, one that has called forth those human faculties which have to do not only with reason and wisdom but also with dialogue, and therefore with all verbal and auditory communication and their media. A fundamental text for this deepening of human nature is found in the literal translation of Ps. 40.6, 'ears thou hast dug for me', or as rendered in the King James Version, 'mine ears thou hast opened'.

Now the New Testament contains particular literary forms such as the 'gospel' and the 'epistle', or the 'parable' and 'canticle', each

---

[1] The codex was used in the Church as early as AD 100 or even earlier: C. H. Roberts, 'The Christian Book and the Greek Papyri', *JTS*, 50 (1949), ff. 155–68; E. J. Goodspeed, *Christianity Goes to Press* (New York 1940). The latter writes: 'In Christianity the literature of religion and the life of faith were linked . . . Christian books were copied and distributed on a scale that no other ancient writings remotely approached' (p. 32). 'The early Christians were to an unusual extent a book-buying and book-reading people. They were also a translating and publishing people' (p. 76). See also B. Gerhardsson, *Memory and Manuscript* (Uppsala 1961), pp. 201–2.

[2] '[Schleiermacher] regarded Christianity, especially in its Western branch, as the religious community that above all others has cultivated an interest in its own language. On the one hand . . . it seemed to him that Christianity presupposes for its propagation a relatively advanced stage of linguistic culture; while, on the other hand, it has also shown itself from the very beginning to be *a language-forming agency*'—R. R. Niebuhr, 'Schleiermacher: Theology as Human Reflection', *HTR* 55/1 (January 1962), p. 28. For the last point the author cites Schleiermacher's *Sendschreiben*, section 60.

of them more or less distinctive if not novel. The significance of these
written or oral speech-forms is greater than may appear at first sight.
Attention to them leads naturally to comparison with the forms and
genres of other literatures, especially of that period, and to the
factors that determined their emergence. Where did such a writing-
form as a 'gospel' come from? What analogies or precedents are
there for such a peculiar literary-form as we find in the Book of
Revelation? Why did they and some other early Christian types
vanish so soon? But our interest here in these early Christian rhetorical
modes goes deeper. Behind the particular New Testament forms lies
a particular life-experience and a language-shaping faith. Our study
of the literary form of the New Testament will throw light on the
faith they carry and the sources of that faith.

III

Jesus of Nazareth and his first followers broke into the world of
speech and writing of their time, and, indeed, into its silence, with
a novel and powerful utterance, that is, with a 'word', and the word
of a layman. Ignatius of Antioch states the matter in his own surrealist style:

> Jesus Christ, his son, who is his word proceeding from silence (*Ad
> Magn.* 8.2),

> He is the mouth which cannot lie, by which the Father has spoken
> truly (*Ad Rom.* 8.2).

Just on the secular level note how significant this was and has been.
At least there was here a new dynamics in human speech. One
thinks of what John Keats said about 'the indescribable gusto of the
Elizabethan voice'. But one searches for more significant analogies.
It is a question of a word from the depths, with power. One analogy
would be that of the man who stands up when a panic is spreading
in a theatre or a riot in the streets and recalls men to their true selves
by a compelling word of authority. But this new word in Israel
initiated a new world of meaning that went on spreading through
ancient society. Here an analogy would be that of the impact of
Dante's use of his vernacular dialect rather than Latin upon the
spiritual culture of Europe. One can think also of the train of consequences that ensued upon the writing by the teenager Arthur Rim-
baud of his *Bateau ivre*. This new spring of symbolist incantation
determined much of the history of modern poetic utterance.

Thus we can understand the sense in which Ernst Fuchs has called the rise of the Gospel a 'speech-event' (*Sprachereignis*). By this he means a new departure, not just in the sense of a new religious teaching, but rather the opening up of a new dimension of man's awareness, a new breakthrough in language and symbolization. He can also say that the Gospel represented a renewal of myth in Israel and the ancient world. The new enlargement of language took on ever new articulation in the course of the Apostolic Age.

To quote Professor Fuchs further:

> Primitive Christianity is itself a speech-phenomenon. It is for that very reason that it established a monument in the new style-form which we call a 'gospel'. The Johannine apocalypse and, indeed, in the first instance the apostolic epistle-literature, these are creations of a new utterance which changes everything that it touches.[1]

He adds that it is only on the margin of the New Testament that one can observe direct assimiliation of pagan rhetoric, as for example in the Pastoral Epistles and in post-canonical writings; at a time, that is, when ecclesiastical patterns had begun to solidify.

Early Christianity, of course, brought forth new forms not only in language but in life itself, not only in writing but in ritual. One could say the same thing about other religions. But the spoken and written word have a basic role in the Christian faith. We note the background for this in the Old Testament. The religion of Israel is very much a matter of hearing rather than of seeing.[2] Even God's actions are spoken of by the prophets as his word. No man can see God and live, but he is known in his speaking. By contrast it is the gods of the nations that are mute, and their visible images are dumb.[3] As we

---

[1] 'Die Sprache im Neuen Testament', *Zur Frage nach dem historischen Jesus* (Tübingen 1960), p. 261.

[2] 'Die Sprache des Alten Testamentes ist hörende Sprache', Zimmerli, *op. cit.*, p. 20. 'For the Hebrew, the decisive reality of the world of experience was the word; for the Greek it was the *thing* . . . we can conclude that for the Hebrew the most important of his senses for the experience of truth was his hearing (as well as various kinds of feeling), but for the Greek it had to be his sight; or perhaps inversely, because the Greeks were organized in a predominantly visual way and the Hebrews in a predominantly auditory way, each people's conception of truth was formed in increasingly different ways. . . . Since both our chief senses, sight and hearing, must pay for their astonishing accomplishments the price of an externally stamped bias, both highly developed peoples of ancient times, Hellas and Israel, could achieve their magnificent contributions to civilization only in virtue of their bias'—Thorleif Boman, *Hebrew Thought Compared with Greek* (London and Philadelphia 1960), pp. 206–7.

[3] Hab. 2.18–19; Ps. 115.5, 7; Isa. 46.7; Jer. 10.5.

read in Ps. 115.7, 'They do not make a sound in their throat.'
Throughout Scripture, revelation is identified above all with speaking and hearing, with writing and reading, with colloquies and
recitals, with tablets and scrolls and parchments, rather than with
the imagery of the visual arts. Even visions are converted into writing: 'Write the vision,' we read in Hab. 2.2; and, 'write what you
see in a book', in Rev. 1.11. The seer, indeed, seems to confuse the
senses when he speaks of seeing the voice or of the 'little scroll' which
he was bidden to eat which was 'as sweet as honey' in his mouth
(10.10). Of course, like all religions Christianity has its sacred actions
and spectacles, sacred places and times, sacred arts and objects, but
it is in connection with God speaking that they are sacred.

It is intriguing to classify religions or even Christian groups according as they assign priority to auditory or visual images. On the
one hand we have religion identified with word and answer; on the
other with vision and ecstasy or metamorphosis. The New Testament
speaks of the divine apprehension in terms of all the senses, not only
hearing and sight but touch and smell (this last in the form of incense
and fragrant odours). Yet the hearing mode is primary. The spirit
may be rapt in vision, but it is with the heart that man hears the
word of faith and with his mouth that he confesses and is saved
(Rom. 10.8–10). Language, then, is more fundamental than graphic
representation, except where the latter is itself a transcript in some
sense of the word of God. In this connection it is interesting to note
what a psychologist writes about the determination of human consciousness by language.

> 'Reality' becomes a meaningful part of consciousness only through the
> interpretation of reality-contacts by language. The importance of
> auditory experiences for the interpretation of reality is proven through
> observation of deaf children. . . . A world without sound is a dead
> world: when sound is eliminated from our experience, it becomes clear
> how inadequate and ambiguous is the visual experience if not accompanied by auditory interpretation. . . . Vision alone without acoustic
> perceptions does not provide understanding. Deaf persons are prone
> to paranoid interpretations of outside events.[1]

In this light it is significant that the emotional dynamics of the
Gospel were always controlled by the meaningfulness of speech. To
this, visionary and psychic phenomena were subordinated. And the

---

[1] Clemens E. Benda, 'Language, Consciousness and Problems of Existential
Analysis (Daseinsanalyse)', American Journal of Psychotherapy 14/2 (April 1960), p. 262.

language in question was not only the spoken word but personal address; it was not only in the indicative mode but in the imperative; it was not only in the third person but in the second and the first; it was not only a matter of declaration but of dialogue.

We can, therefore, appreciate the special incentives to the literary arts that Christianity has always provided, just as other faiths have provided special incentives to the visual arts or to music and dancing. Christianity is a religion of the Book and this has had its corollaries for its total cultural thrust.[1] It is true that when the Church took over the heritage of classical culture—ancient rhetoric, architecture, painting and sculpture—it related itself to all the arts and has exploited them all ever since in changing situations. But the thesis still holds that the faith identifies itself fundamentally with the arts of hearing as against those of sight and touch. Even when the Christian paints or carves or dances or sings he does so to a text, and identifies himself with an archetypal dialogue between God and man.

Even so far as the literary arts themselves are in view—arts which have, of course, come to consummate expression in many religious traditions—one could argue that particular genres are at home both in the Church and in particular Christian cultures of different periods. Erich Auerbach has studied the peculiar forms and styles of biblical and post-biblical Christian narrative forms as compared with classical.[2] Martin Jarrett-Kerr has presented illustrations in different periods of Western literature of the special morphology of writings of Christian inspiration.[3] One can also say that the novel as it has evolved in the modern period is a form which is only possible in a world whose view of man and society has been shaped by Christian presupposition.

IV

Throughout our analysis we shall find ourselves recurring to one feature of the *earliest* Christian speech including that of Jesus. It is naïve, it is not studied; it is *extempore* and directed to the occasion, it

---

[1] A poignant example of the Christian book-lover is St Jerome, who writes as follows in his twenty-second letter: 'Many years ago for the sake of the Kingdom of Heaven I cut myself off from home, parents, sister, relations, and, what was harder, from the dainty food to which I had been used. But even when I was on my way to Jerusalem to fight the good fight there, I could not bring myself to forgo the library which with great care and labour I had gotten together at Rome.'

[2] *Mimesis: the Representation of Reality in Western Literature* (Princeton 1953).

[3] *Studies in Literature and Belief* (London: Rockliff, n.d.).

is not calculated to serve some future hour. This utterance is dynamic, actual, immediate, reckless of posterity; not coded for catechists or repeaters. It is only one aspect of this that it is oral and not written. We find ourselves at first and for a rather long time in the presence of oral and live face-to-face communication. The Gospel meant freedom of speech in this deeper sense. One did not hoard its formulas, since when occasion arose the Spirit would teach one what to say and how to witness and what defence to make. The earliest Christians lived on the free bounty of God in this sense also. The speech of the Gospel was thus fresh and its forms novel and fluid; it came and went, as Ernst Fuchs says, with the freedom of sunshine, wind and rain.

Even the writing forms of the Early Church are better understood if we keep in mind the primal role of oral speech in the beginning. *Viva voce* communication is more malleable, more personal and more searching. These qualities were to distinguish Christian discourse even when it was obliged to take on written form. So far as we know Jesus never wrote a word, except on that occasion when, in the presence of the woman taken in adultery, 'he bent down and wrote with his finger on the ground'.[1] In secular terms we could say that Jesus spoke as the birds sing, oblivious of any concern for transcription. Less romantically we can say that Jesus' use of the spoken word alone has its own theological significance. For one thing speaking is more direct than writing, and we would expect this in him through whom God openly staged his greatest controversy with his people. The transaction in which Jesus was involved was neither more nor less than a trial, and the parties in a trial confront each other in direct confrontation, as in Jesus' parables of the talents and the sheep and the goats. Jesus was a voice not a penman, a herald not a scribe, a watchman with his call in the market-place and the Temple, and not a cry[2] of alarm in the wilderness like John the Baptist. This deportment of Jesus is a sign. We are reminded of the acted parables of certain of the prophets of earlier times: one of whom went naked as a token of slavery to come; and one of whom was eloquently dumb for a period. In Israel's tradition God's servants the prophets did not write unless they were ordered to, however it might be with the scribes.

[1] Possibly, it is suggested, in line with the practice of judges of the time, who first wrote, then read, their decision.

[2] Cf. Ignatius of Antioch, who contrasts his own role of being a 'word of God' (if he dies as a martyr) with being 'only a cry' (if he is spared): *Ad Rom.* 2.1.

That Jesus confined himself to the spoken and precarious word is of a piece with his renunciation of all cultural bonds such as home and trade and property; and with his instruction to his disciples to 'take nothing for their journey except a staff; no bread, no bag, no money in their belts; but to wear sandals and not to put on two tunics' (Mark 6.8–9). This deportment has its true significance in the crisis with which Jesus was identified. For him and his generation history was fractured, time's course was in dissolution, continuities were broken. The act of writing presupposes continuities and a future. Jesus' word was for the present, the last hour. Indeed, his whole manifestation was a presence. This observation agrees with Günther Bornkamm's thesis in his *Jesus of Nazareth*.[1] The Judaism of the time looked back to the Lawgiver and the covenants, and forward to the time of salvation. In so doing, the contemporaries of Jesus forfeited the present.[2] Jesus brought both the will of God and the promises of God into the present with inexorable sharpness and actuality. Only the living voice can serve such an occasion.

Professor Fuchs makes this observation that Jesus wrote nothing and adds that even Paul wrote reluctantly. When he and other authors of our New Testament writings *did* write or dictate, their speech still has a special character, since the new depth and freedom of speech perpetuated itself even in the written productions. The voice of the writer is the voice of the speaker to a remarkable degree.

Paul wrote reluctantly and in any case without an extended historical perspective. He saw himself in the situation of harvester of the last days (Rom. 1.18), and as vocal herald of a world-crisis, as is suggested in the passage he cites from Psalm 16:

> Their voice has gone out to all the earth
> And their words to the ends of the world.[3]

Paul writes always as one thwarted by absence and eagerly anticipating meeting or reunion. He is distressed by circumstances which prevent face-to-face address: 'I could wish to be present with you now,' he writes to the Galatians, 'and change my tone, for I am perplexed about you' (4.20). Even in writing he falls into the style of direct oral plea and challenge. The very nature of the Gospel imposes

[1] London and New York 1960, p. 58.
[2] *Ibid.*, p. 55.
[3] Rom. 10.18.

upon him ways of expression that suggest dramatic immediacy: devices and rhythms of the speaker rather than the writer; imagined dialogue; the situation of a court hearing or church trial with its accusations and defences; the use of direct discourse; challenges not so much to understand the written words but to listen and behold; queries, exclamations and oaths.

To return to the sayings of Jesus. It is true that we do have evidence that his words and deeds were carried in memory and reported. We find such statements in the Gospels as the following: 'At that time Herod the tetrarch heard about the fame of Jesus' (Matt. 14.1); or, 'so his fame spread throughout all Syria' (Matt. 4.24). But we should make a distinction between an inevitable live diffusion of Jesus' words, on the one hand, and formal memorization or writing down of what he said, on the other. Some scholars hold that Jesus taught much as the scribes did with a view to the learning by heart of his words and deeds as though for catechetical use among his disciples.[1] They have a plausible argument in the poetic and formal structure of much of his utterance. They even speak of mnemonic devices employed: parallelism, assonance, chiasmus and various scribal patterns of pronouncement. But all this ignores the radical difference between Jesus and the Jewish teachers, the eschatological outlook of Jesus, who was not schooling his followers in a learned mode for new generations to come, and the intense urging with which he spoke to the immediate crisis and the face-to-face hearer. The incomparable felicity and patterning of his sayings is indeed evident, but this formal perfection is not a matter of mnemonics; it is the countersign of the most effective communication of the moment. Naturally his words and parables were remembered and retold, often with great accuracy, so lucid and inevitable was his phrasing. But here as always the new speech of the Gospel was not a matter of words on a tablet but a word in the heart, not a copybook for recitation but winged words for life.

Now immediately we must add that this extempore character of the early Christian voice did not continue indefinitely, though in a sense it must always continue.[2] The uncalculating oral speech and

---

[1] H. Riesenfeld, 'The Gospel Tradition and its Beginnings', *The Gospels Reconsidered* (Oxford 1960), pp. 147–53; B. Gerhardsson, *Memory and Manuscript*, pp. 328–9.

[2] On the essentially oral character of the Gospel Luther's words are striking. 'In the New Testament the proclamation should take place by word of mouth,

dialogue of Jesus and his first followers gave place in part to memorization and repetition, and eventually to writing and later to the greater formality of publication. But even when the face-to-face rhetorical forms of the beginnings gave way to the conventionality of written records and letters, these are still characterized by a perennially dramatic element which goes back to the very nature of the Christian religion. The Christian styles tend to evoke or restore the face-to-face encounter. The new utterance of the Gospel can never settle comfortably into any fixtures of formula or print or book, though with new cultural situations it can shape these also in a way to safeguard the immediacies of faith. Here is one of the touchstones not only of Christian literature but of the Christian arts generally. At their core is the divine action and covenant-dialogue, and this distinguishes them from pagan and secular celebrations.

As the epigraph to this chapter we have cited the words of Ignatius:

Jesus Christ, his son, who is his word proceeding from silence.

The early Christian rhetoric was a new speech from the depths. There is a striking parallel to this saying by the poet Rilke. He speaks of

the uninterrupted news that grows out of silence.

---

publicly in an animated tone, and should bring that forward into speech and hearing which before was hidden in the letters and in apparent concealment. Since the New Testament is none other than an opening up and disclosure of the Old Testament . . . therefore it is that Christ himself did not write his own teaching as Moses did his, but gave it forth by word of mouth and commanded that it should be done orally and gave no commandment to write it. . . . Before [the apostles] wrote, they preached and converted men by their living presence and voice. . . . That books had to be written was already a great departure and breach with the Spirit, occasioned by necessity, and not in keeping with the New Testament.'

The above is cited by Gerhard Ebeling in his article, 'Wort Gottes und Hermeneutik', ZTK 56 (1959), pp. 231–2 [ET in *Word and Faith* (London 1963), pp. 312–13]. His own comment is very much to the point of our argument: 'Luther had at heart here his insight into different speech-modes (*um die Einsicht in differente Möglichkeiten des Sprachgeschehens*), especially as they relate to the difference between law and Gospel. [As he wrote, contrasting the Gospel with the law:] "But the Gospel is entrusted to the living and untrammelled voice, poured forth to the ears of men, and therefore has more vigour to the end of conversion." [In biblical orthodoxy which exalts the *written* Word] it is no longer recognized that this oral feature inheres in the very nature of the Word of God, that is, its nature as an event in personal relations; and that the Word, therefore, is not just a bearer of a certain content of meaning which can be isolated, but a happening which brings something to pass and moves towards what it has in view.'

It is admirable how Rilke independently touches the same mystery, though in the aesthetic domain. And it illuminates the Christian word. For it brings out on the one hand the miraculous unedited newness of the word, breaking forth out of silence, out of ignorance, out of nescience. And it also brings out the flowing character of that word as 'uninterrupted news'—the speech of the Gospel that renews itself and conveys life from generation to generation from inexhaustible fountains.

II

MODES AND GENRES

They will speak in new tongues.

MARK 16.17

W E HAVE SEEN that the coming of the Christian Gospel was in one aspect a renewal and liberation of language. It was a 'speech-event', the occasion for a new utterance and new forms of utterance, and eventually new kinds of writing. As Christ declares to the eleven disciples after his Resurrection, in a scene added at the close of our Gospel of Mark: 'these signs will accompany those who believe . . . they will speak in new tongues' (16.17).

We turn now to consider some of the features of this new phenomenon. Before we identify forms and patterns, however, we call attention to a number of wider observations. In fact, there are some aspects of the early Christian discourse and literature that are so obvious that their significance is not always recognized.

I

In the first place it is not just a truism to observe that Jesus spoke in Aramaic and that Paul and the later evangelists spoke and wrote in the Greek *koine* of the Roman world. The founders of Christianity used the languages and idioms of the people: not a sacred or holy language, nor a learned language, nor did they encourage an ecstatic language. Similarly with respect to styles and forms: these were not esoteric, either in the sense of Jewish or Hellenistic *arcana*, or holy formulas. It is true that the Old Testament was cherished and cited as the Word of God, but with an extraordinary freedom. The languages and idioms used by the Christians were those of the wide publics of their time and place. The Christians renewed these in various ways and modified their vocabularies, but there was no flight from the vernacular. Christian utterance and writing did have charismatic power and revelatory prestige, but not in the sense of esoteric holy texts. The common language of men was itself the medium of revelation.

This tension between the novelty of the Gospel and the language patterns of mankind manifested itself in the earliest Church in one striking phenomenon, that of *glossolalia* or "speaking with tongues'. Here the believers were so carried out of themselves that they felt impelled to transcend human language and to commune in the language of angels or other mantic articulation. Since language is such a fundamental socio-cultural activity we have here a striking indication of the eschatological consciousness of the Gospel. But it is significant that this mode of speech was strictly controlled or discouraged in the Early Church. A number of intriguing corollaries of this phenomenon suggest themselves.

We note for one thing that Jesus himself shows no inclination in this direction, despite the radicalness of his eschatology. Many of his sayings reflect the charismatic mood and even visionary experience. But passion in him used the common speech and did not dissolve it. His human self-identification with his fellows evidences itself here, too, in the matter of speech. In the case of Paul the alternative of ecstatic speech is explicitly faced, and we know that he disparaged it. He modified the various modes of communication which he used, imparting the gifts bestowed by God in words 'taught by the Spirit' (I Cor. 2.13), yet he did not depart from the vernacular speech of the Empire. What we can say is that the new rhetorical power of the Gospel forced new styles upon current usage and idiom, and we have here a parable of the Christian arts throughout the centuries.

The Bible gives almost no support to the idea of a special 'holy language', as, for example, Latin in the piety or liturgy of the Church, or by analogy some supposed specially holy translation of the Bible. Jesus taught in the living dialect of his time, Aramaic, not in the language of the Scripture, Hebrew. The early Church had no hesitation in translating his words into Greek or into the language of whatever population was evangelized: Latin, Syriac, Coptic, etc.[1]

The idea of a holy language was similarly unknown to ancient Israel and only emerged in Judaism in a struggle against assimilation. The plurality of tongues in the wider world was seen in the

[1] Brief Aramaic phrases carried over into the Greek of the New Testament, whether of Jesus himself or of the Church (*Marana-tha*, I Cor. 16.22) have each their special explanation.

older tradition as a blessing: so many languages, so many blessings (Gen. 10). The later tradition of the Tower of Babel, indeed, sees the many tongues as a curse (Gen. 11). By this time Israel was the prey of great empires made up of men of 'strange lips'. After the return from exile Hebrew inevitably became one of the defences of the Jews against assimilation (cf. Neh. 13.23–25). The climax of this tendency is reflected in the later rabbinic view that the future world is only for those who command the holy language, i.e. Hebrew.[1] But this attitude is not reflected in the post-exilic writings of the Old Testament as a whole.

The early Christian speech favoured no particular language. We can extend this to say that it offers no precedents for what is sometimes spoken of as the 'language of Zion', that is, a particular vocabulary and imagery thought of as sacred or pious. It is true that faith nourishes itself upon biblical and inherited expressions and images. But when these take on a fixed or magical character their meaning is forfeited. Zimmerli provides an Old Testament precedent. The repertory of images used in the prophets and the old tradition of Israel—such images for Israel as the vine or vineyard, the foundling or orphan, the wife—these were not allowed to become a 'holy language' or stereotypes in the post-exilic writers. They were continually reshaped and combined with new and fresh figures and expressions.[2] The new utterance which Jesus and his followers brought into the world similarly re-created the religious vocabulary of the Old Testament. The Early Church for its part relayed the words and deeds of Jesus not by a mere anachronistic repetition but by a combination of his words and imagery with new variations and new resources of all kinds. Thus whether as regards language as tongue or language as imagery and diction there should be no such thing as a 'language of Zion'. There is, indeed, such a thing as a rhetoric of faith, the language of the Spirit; one can recognize that the early Christians were endowed with new tongues; but all such heavenly discourse remains rooted in the secular media of ordinary speech. Pentecost, indeed, we may take as a dramatization of the fact that there is no peculiar Christian tongue.

II

There is a second obvious aspect of the early Christian speech and

[1] Cf. Sota 7.1–5 and see Zimmerli, p. 2.
[2] Op. cit., p. 19.

writing which does not receive the attention it should have, and which repays examination. The topic may, at first appear surprising. It is the question of quantity, of volume, of length, not only of the New Testament itself, and not only of the various writings within it, but of the older oral speech-forms behind the writings. It is not by accident that the Gospels are as long or as short as they are, or the Book of Acts, or the sermon-epistles like Hebrews, or the prayers, hymns, parables, etc. Why is the shipwreck journey of Paul told at considerable length while the important Passion narrative is relatively short? Why are so few aspects of the life of Jesus included when, as we are told in the Gospel of John, 'There are many other things that Jesus did; were every one of them to be written, I suppose that the world itself could not contain the books that would be written' (21.25)?

We can only touch upon this topic, but it is evident that we learn something here about the early Christian speech and rhetoric. At least we can say that it was not diffuse or verbose. As one of the early Christian Fathers said, Christianity was not talk. Perhaps a good part of the question is covered if we say that the words relayed and written were those given to the witnesses and not what they spoke for themselves. But the question goes deeper than this. It would be relevant to compare other religions with respect to the extent of verbal material from their early period, their prolixity: Islam and its Koran, for example; or even the literary phenomena of Mormonism or Christian Science.

There are some things that are said by scholars that bear on our question. An ordinary papyrus scroll of about thirty feet would be about right for one of our longer Gospels, Matthew or Luke, or for the Book of Acts. But were the evangelists determined by such a mechanical consideration? The Gospel of Mark is not much more than half the length of Luke. Our Christian apocalypse of John is about half the length of the Ezra apocalypse in the Apocrypha. Ecclesiasticus, by the way, is much longer than any of our New Testament writings.

We must believe that the length of any early Christian text was fundamentally determined by what the message called for in the given situation or the needs of instruction or exhortation. The basic character of the Gospel, however, is revelation, not persuasion. Persuasion may take a great deal of talk and argument, revelation does not. Yet the occasion of a testimony would always be a factor. Here a kind of early Christian sociology becomes relevant. We would not expect that the whole of a Gospel would be read at a single meeting of a church in the Apostolic Age. Neither do we think, as some hold, that the Gospels were written on the basis of particular lections for particular days of the church year. Neither do we think that the format of, say, Mark was shaped on the precedent of a Greek tragedy. It is possible that the length of the two parts of Luke-Acts was in part conditioned by pagan precedents. But the length of Mark, and this is the crucial matter, was determined kerygmatically to the end of revelation, not of biography and not of instruction. It is its length that needs to be explained, not its brevity. Mark writes what is necessary to be grasped as to the way *with* Christ through humiliation to glory. This is less in the genre of a history than of a re-enactment, a devotional triptych or series of panels. Therefore it is brief in words but dense in import. The best analogy to the brevity of the Gospels is the brevity of Jesus' own career. The drama of God's action in Christ, chronologically considered, was brief; only a few months. Geographically considered it was also very restricted. What was crucial was the depth and not the external dimensions. The literary character of our oldest Gospel corresponds. Here, too, the new speech-forms of this new people corresponded to the Word of God, that is, his action.

The question as to length or amplitude of the early Christian rhetoric may be raised also with reference to the oral traditions that lie behind our writings. It does not always follow that brevity is the test of significance. It may be recalled that one of the features of the Bible that is praised in the 'Preface to the Readers' of the King James Version is its 'fullness'. By this they must have had the Old Testament especially in view, and the concrete and detailed presentation of so many sides of life. This biblical humanism with its corresponding rhetorical features in saga and recital is not present in anything like the same degree in the New Testament. Of course, much of the Old Testament narrative can be broken down into older brief units and stories, and these correspond to the short separate anecdotes that lie behind our Gospels or the short hymns and confessions that are cited in the Epistles. But the later editors of Israel gathered up the older material into long cycles or collections while the Christian authors at most brought together short series of sayings like the Sermon on the Mount or a collection of parables or miracles in the course of the writing of the Gospels.

The New Testament—if we set aside the Apocalypse as a special case—is remarkably free from the plerophoric style or the kinds of preciosity current in the day among pagans, whether the so-called Asiatic pompousness or the pseudo-Attic. Our attention is, of course, specially called to the sayings of Jesus and his parables to which we shall return later. For our text we may take his words of warning against heaping up 'empty phrases as the Gentiles' (Matt. 6.7), or against idle oaths and protestations (Matt. 5.34–37; 23.16–22).

The fact is that the new speech of the Gospel represented not only a liberation but also a purification of language, and not only with respect to falsehood but also to emptiness and hollowness. In the Old Testament we note not only appreciation of the gift of apt speech, and not only a sense of the curse of the confusion of tongues but also a sense of the burden of so much human speech in its vanity. The author of Ecclesiastes groans at the weariness of it, but recognizes that man's addiction to it is insatiable! Professor Zimmerli deals interestingly with this theme.[1] Wilhelm von Humboldt in a wide-ranging discussion of the significance of the diversity of languages in the world had noted the boundlessness of man's loquacity, the sheer energy that goes into speech, as evidence of the richness of the human spirit. Ecclesiastes is deeply disturbed by this.

> All words wear themselves out;
> a man cannot utter it;
> the eye is not satisfied with seeing,
> nor the ear filled with hearing (1.8).[2]

His only recourse is to insist that there is

> a time to keep silence, and a time to speak,

just as in Proverbs tells us: 'a word in season, how good it is!'

But emptiness or non-sense in speech is closely akin to falsehood. Now the comparative brevity of the early Christian speech-forms is related to both. Besides Jesus' warnings against 'much speaking' and even the contrast in his parable of the Pharisee and the Publican, we can set Paul's disavowal of 'lofty' and 'plausible' words not to mention his bridling of ecstatic tongues. But we also have an example of the 'purification of the language of the tribe' evident in many of the speech-forms of the Early Church. Jesus himself

[1] Zimmerli, *op. cit.*, p. 6.
[2] For translation, *ibid.*

spoke in short aphorisms and oracles and tightly knit parables, but also, we may say, in silences. The writings of the later followers are not discursive even in their homiletic sections. The utterance in its many modes was economical just because it was urgent and faithful. Even when it was elevated, its syntactical and prosodic forms were free from prolixity and from rhetoric in the bad sense. We may find an analogy in the observation made by a contemporary writer contrasting two poems, one by Friedrich Hölderlin and one by Rilke:

> The Hölderlin is beyond praise. What 'toughness' or terrible strength in his syntax and rhythms, and omission of connectives. Rilke trying to be orphic cannot stand beside it.[1]

III

In turning now to specific forms and genres we should have in mind a number of considerations bearing on the analysis. We have observed that the particular topic of these chapters is not so much what the early Christians said as how they said it. Yet these two matters cannot finally be separated, as every student of literature and art knows.

The very idea of form in art or religion is one that we need to be cautious about. We should not confuse form proper with externals, or style with ornamentation. It is suspicious that it is only when form is misused that our attention is specially drawn to it. In such cases we speak of mannerism or preciosity. In the period of the New Testament we see examples of this among pagan writers. From the time of Alexander on much Greek writing either took on a mannered imitation of the older Attic models or affected an Asiatic novelty featured by deliberate mystification, novel rhythms and showy word-plays. New Testament authors like Paul were not even tempted by these styles, though there are differences among them as regards literary sophistication. Yet in a church like that at Corinth there were those who felt the appeal of some forms of popular Hellenistic rhetoric as we know from Paul's defence of his style. As Eduard Norden observed, Paul abjured 'eloquent wisdom' and 'lofty words' 'at a time when the art of speech was everything and no wisdom could dispense with it, especially in writing to citizens of a metropolis in which as is well known, rhetoric was highly favoured.'[2]

---

[1] Thornton Wilder, in a letter.
[2] *Die antike Kunstprosa* II (Leipzig 1898), p. 493.

Our attention is not usually drawn to form apart from matter in the case of true works of art. The shape of an axe handle or of an airplane is determined, as we say, by function. The shape or build of an honest poem or prayer is inseparable from its import. When we do find works of art or literature in which the form calls attention to itself, or when we find critics presupposing a systematic distinction, both artist and critic are under the influence of one or other philosophy like idealism which sees the world in two layers such as mind and matter, or spirit and flesh. Such dualism is alien to Hebraism and Christianity and the 'forms' we are concerned with in the Early Church are not conditioned by such a world-view. In the Greek vocabulary of the New Testament the terms translated 'form', 'likeness' and 'image' (*morphē, schēma, eikōn*) usually refer not to the external appearance but to the total reality of the person or thing in question[1]. This kind of holistic thinking is confirmed in our modern philosophy and aesthetics by our better knowledge today and appreciation of primitive art, as well as by modern psychology. In all genuine artifacts, including language-forms, shape and substance are inseparable and mutually determinative.

In this light there are two observations to make about the forms of the early Christian literature. In the first place they are evidently deeply determined by the faith or life-orientation that produced them. We have already spoken in our first lecture of the way in which different cultures bring forth different arts. The culture-outlook that produced the forms assigned to Confucius was different from that which lay behind the Vedic hymns. This thesis can be stated negatively. Some cultures do not and cannot produce certain literary forms. The older literature of India illustrates this point. Corresponding to the lack of concern with history is an absence of certain genres of literature such as personal poetry or poetry of national interest. This observation bears upon the period after the Brahmanic philosophy developed. This point is discussed by Martin Jarrett-Kerr in his *Studies in Literature and Belief*[2] in dependence on the work of specialists. Personal poetry, national epic, real drama,

[1] See R. Bultmann, *Theology of the New Testament* I (New York 1951), pp. 192–3. There are exceptions where the dualistic associations of the terms in pagan Greek are carried over in the interests of *ad hoc* argument.

[2] Pages 13–14. Note that recognition is given to the original epic material later taken up into the *Mahabharata* and *Ramayana* and to the 'moments of vivid writing in the *Gita*' which, however, 'are almost at once swallowed up into the Upanishadic philosophy which the poem, as we have it, is designed to convey'.

tragedy: these all presuppose a fateful sense of irreversible and eventful history.

To give one example from the Early Church: the style of the Fourth Gospel and the design of parts of it, as, for example, the farewell discourses, are governed by a world-view very different from that which lies behind the other Gospels and are related to an outlook which produced a variety of Gnostic literary forms.[1] The most obvious features in common are the oracular antithetical deliverances of Christ, the ceremonial 'I am' sayings, and the peculiar dialogue features in which the opposition of truth and ignorance is contrasted. Apart from style itself, we can add that the images and mythical material used testify to the same background.

Secondly, the rhetorical forms we are concerned with are not only governed by general world-view but also by particular social patterns. Whether the single aphorism or parable of Jesus, or the gospel-genre, or the shape and compass of the New Testament canon as a whole, all these language-phenomena are the deposit of a movement: community-products. They severally reflect various aspects of the emergence of a new society in the world of that time, a new race as it was later called. Inevitably its literary patterns were or became distinctive as in the case of its social patterns. Of particular interest is the relation of many of these rhetorics to worship-situations. One point at which the contribution of the form-critics is unassailable is their demonstration of the cult-context of many of the small paragraphs in the Synoptic Gospels. The same is true of quoted elements now embedded in the Epistles. The Gospels themselves, to use a technical term that has no disparaging connotations, are 'cult-legends', that is, they set forth the story of salvation as contemplated and re-enacted in prayer and worship. All in all, these early Christian styles, these voices, oracles and texts, all bear the marks of the forge of the new fellowship and of the Spirit, whether in the dynamic privacy of their meetings or in the external activities of the mission.

To suggest the way in which special groups produce their own rhetorics one could cite the Negro spirituals and slave songs. The basic stock of these came out of the second quarter of the nineteenth century. While they are distinctive and inimitable, the literary and musical historian can show their antecedents in the general hymnology of the period and the chants and rhythms of the African

---

[1] Heinz Becker, *Die Reden des Johannesevangeliums und der Stil der gnostischen Offenbarungsrede* (Göttingen 1956), p. 57.

tribesmen. This art form is the product of a group although initiated surely in every case by some unknown individual. They are also cult-songs, fostered and shaped in the recurrent secret assemblies of the slaves, a Christian continuation of the ceremonies they had brought with them from Africa. Their oral, ·anonymous and un-literary character offers a significant parallel to primitive Christian utterance. A further feature goes far to complete the parallel. The texts of the slave songs not only varied from region to region, but from decade to decade. In fact, the successive versions of a given slave song reflected the actual changed circumstances of the Negroes, just as we can recognize adaptations and overlays in early Christian traditions. These features of the history of the slave songs have been documented by Professor Mark Miles Fisher.[1] He shows that successive public events and policies significant for the situation and hopes of the slaves brought about revisions in the texts of the songs. Thus this body of cult-songs went through the same sort of form-history as the contents of the Jewish Psalter or the early Christian stories, hymns and testimonies.

When we take up the New Testament we note immediately four different literary types: gospel, acts, letter, and apocalypse. Even so we are influenced by titles to the writings that were added subsequently. The Gospels actually do not call themselves by this term. The opening words of Mark use it in another sense. 'The beginning of the gospel of Jesus Christ' means—'The beginning of the Good News', not the beginning of a gospel in the sense of a kind of book. The Acts of the Apostles does not give itself a title or a category. In fact, it originally followed Luke as the second part of a double work. On a closer view we find that some of the letters in the New Testament are not really letters. The Book of Revelation does actually call itself in the first verse a 'revelation', in the sense, however, of a vision rather than a literary form.

When we look within the writings we may with varying degrees of assurance recognize certain formal patterns especially if our printed editions help us by typographical guides. Thus we can identify poetry as against prose; an occasional short letter included in the Book of Acts and a group of them in the Book of Revelation; a doxology here, a prayer there; in the Gospels: parables, anecdotes, dialogues, genealogies. We also note various listings of apostles, of Old Testament figures, of nations, of virtues and vices; or groupings

[1] *Negro Slave Songs in the United States* (Ithaca: Cornell University Press 1953).

of beatitudes, of parables, of miracles; also various number schemes, and serial arrangements, for example of age-categories, or of domestic and social relationships: parents and children, masters and slaves, rulers and subjects; and various other forms and patterns.

One indication of the originality of the primitive Christian literature appears in the difficulty we have in finding terms for all such forms. The very word 'literature' is unsatisfactory, as is so often evident in books on the Bible 'as literature'. The term 'poetry' as we ordinarily use it has to be carefully qualified when we apply it to the rhythmic parts of the Bible. The category of 'biography' is not suitable to the Gospels nor is that of tragedy. The term 'history' is not adequate for the Book of Acts, nor is 'oratory' appropriate to the discourses of the apostles or the prophets. Our usual tools for rhetorical genres and forms are at home in the classical and humanist traditions, but come short when we face our present task.

All the literary forms of the New Testament, even those that may seem to have a pagan background, fall definitely outside the categories of formal literature as practised in the world of culture of that time. This feature has been stated by scholars in a number of different ways. The Christian writings are assigned to the class of *Kleinliteratur* rather than *Hochliteratur*; that is they are popular texts in the sense of unsophisticated and unliterary. This is also what is meant when they are seen as belonging to the category of *Volksbuch*. Best known is the statement that the Gospels were 'writings of the people, by the people, and for the people', that is, for the unliterary classes of the Roman empire. It is true that there were in the Mediterranean world of that period pagan writings of a popular character. But even here real distinctions can be made.

Let us look more closely at certain of the written forms in our canon and first that of the gospel. This is the only wholly new genre created by the Church and the author of Mark receives the credit for it. Yet this anonymous work is in large degree a group product and rests on the contributions of many unknown transmitters of the evangelical traditions. As a type of composition we have seen that it is not like the ancient biography or tragedy. Dibelius has shown how different it is from narratives, perhaps superficially similar, of the fate of a hero or of the life and death of a saint or martyr. All such accounts were written with an appeal to sentiment, with sharper portraiture or with fuller biographical detail. Mark represents a divine transaction whose import involves heaven and earth, and even the scenes of the Passion are recounted with a corresponding austerity. As we have said, the gospel action is not a history so much as a ritual re-enactment or mimesis. The believer did not hear it as a record of the past. With the brotherhood he found himself in the middle of the world-changing transaction of conflict, death and glory. We have here a new speech-form in the profound sense of a new communication of meaning, by which men could live. Mark offers us the faith-story of Christ as a pattern of meaning or life-orientation for the believer, especially for the Roman Church in a situation of persecution. It presents the 'way' of Christ, the way of life in two successive phases which are yet telescoped, the phase of incognito and abandonment, and the phase of transfiguration.

We make a mistake to think of the four Gospels as all of a type, and even to think of the Synoptic Gospels as similar. They are very different and thus evidence the new enlargement of literary means. The author of Matthew fell heir to Mark's format and to the faith-story behind it, but wove into it other aspects of the Church's concerns. We usually say that Matthew is a well-planned manual of instruction and discipline for a going church-institution, with Christ presented as the authority for the order set forth. But every part of the Gospel comes out of the new powerful faith, mystique and dynamics of this new creation that began through Jesus of Nazareth.

Here it is important to make clear what the formative element is in the largest as in many of the smallest units of the early Christian literature. We speak of it as the Good News. But it is Good News of a total and ultimate kind, and not only recited but effectively and dynamically demonstrated. The simplest versions of it, the Gospel in microcosm, are found in any one of the brief accounts of Jesus' healings or exorcisms. For here we have concrete dramatization of the power of God effecting what is impossible with men. Each such narrative is a pledge of the divine omnipotence in the overruling of evil. The narrative of the passion and resurrection of Christ is the supreme instance of this mystery. Faith takes hold of the actuality of the God who opens a way where there is no way, who breaks the bars of brass, who gives life to the dead and calls into existence the things that do not exist, who chooses things that are not to bring to nothing things that are, who creates a new thing. This is the formative element of the Gospel story in the small and in the large. It determines the basic speech-mode of Christianity which is that of a story, and therefore the Gospel anecdotes, but, of course, especially the Gospels.

The Gospel of Matthew, then, includes many of the smaller instances of the divine fiat, the baring of God's mighty arm, along with the account of Christ's death and exaltation. Along with this are many aspects of the life of the disciple, the missioner, the fellowship, as illuminated by the cosmic action in course of fulfilment. The author of Luke-Acts does something quite different from either Mark or Matthew. For him there is now a real interval of elapsed time since the salvation was manifested by Jesus and since the ascended Christ had conferred the Spirit upon his followers. The author therefore writes a kind of retrospective praeternatural history of the acts of salvation, in two parts. The different points of view from which Matthew and Luke-Acts are written mean that even where they embody the same traditions these are often significantly changed in the reporting. To see these differences one must read these Gospels through at a sitting and notice not only the differences in style but in architecture within and without. One then begins to realize that the Synoptic Gospels differ as much from each other as the Fourth Gospel differs from any or all of them. Different conditions in the different churches from which they variously come underlie the differences in form.

The author of John could have written instead a meditation on the incarnation of the Word, or the visit to this lower world of the heavenly Revealer. Thus we might have had from him not a gospel but a homily like the Coptic Gospel of Truth. But the narrative pattern established by Mark or otherwise known to him imposed itself upon him so that his unique heavenly discourse is presented in the gospel-form; that is, interwoven with a recital of symbolic deeds and dialogues of the historical Christ. As a result we have a kind of sacred drama or oratorio. It is perhaps not surprising that when Dorothy Sayers writes a modern radio-play series on the life of Christ entitled *The Man Born to be King*, the work reminds us most of this Gospel. It is to be noted that none of our four evangelists writes as a self-conscious literary craftsman. Not one of them names himself. Only in Luke-Acts do we find the author using the first person of himself or referring to his method of working. But 'Luke' no more than the others writes biography or history as we find it in ancient lives (*vita*) or memorabilia (*apomnēmoneumata*) or histories. In none of them is there any description of the appearance of the actors, or any attempt to cover the entire life-span of Jesus, least of all his psychology or the motives of his action. The classical writers stood above their material as artists portraying their subjects for the book-trade, while our evangelists are devoutly ordering for local believers the testimonies provided for them by tradition not as a biography but as the cult-story of faith.

IV

When we turn to the Epistles we learn to distinguish between actual letters and discourses written in letter form. Even so there are varieties. The New Testament epistle provides us with a good example of how Christianity took over a familiar literary form and reshaped it creatively. It is all the more interesting in this case because the letter is already such a combination of the conventional and the personal. We all know that a letter can take many forms depending on whether we are writing to intimates or to strangers, to children or to adults, whether we are writing a bread-and-butter letter or a condolence letter or a travel-diary in the form of letters, whether we are writing in our own name or as secretary for some society, whether we are writing a business letter or a scientific communication. The letter was also used in the ancient world as a literary form for general publication as a way of personalizing a composition, and letters were assigned to famous authors as an artistic device. In short the letter as a written form is almost as flexible as oral speech itself, and like direct oral address has an implicit dialogue character.

Since the Gospel itself is personal word and address we can understand that the letter became a favoured form in the Church where oral communication became impossible, and how it came to be used even for other purposes than direct two-party correspondence. To present an exhortation like the Epistle to the Hebrews in the form of a letter, or to write a doxology over the Christian salvation like the Epistle to the Ephesians, was to lend to these an intimate family character, especially when such make-believe letters could include cherished echoes of some great martyr apostle like Peter or Paul.

The letters in the New Testament bring to our attention the whole question of anonymity in early Christian composition. In the case of frescoes in the catacombs there seems to have been a complete lack of interest in the identity of the painter. There was no sense of artistic proprietorship or reputation. These works were naïve and in a sense community products. This same attitude prevailed in the construction of the medieval cathedrals as in the case of the old English ballads. When we turn to the New Testament we find a variety of phenomena here. There are two forms which by their very nature presuppose individual authorship by name yet in different ways, the letter and the apocalypse. The apocalypses, whether Jewish or Christian, were always assigned to a given seer, and so it is with our Book of Revelation or the apocryphal Apocalypse of Peter. But the author named was not the real author, that is, these writings were pseudonymous. This is probably true of our Book of Revelation assigned to the apostle John according to the conventions of this kind of writing. In a similar way the so-called Little Apocalypse in the thirteen chapter of Mark is placed in the mouth of Jesus. But the apocalypse form in the New Testament is basically anonymous. The real author is incognito and all attention is upon the divine communication.

In the case of the letter-form, similarly, we have authorship indicated by name. A letter is not a true letter unless it carries the name of writer and addressee. Thus Paul's genuine letters are highly personal direct communications. But we also have pseudonymous letters, whether of Paul, Peter, James or Jude, and here again the real author remains incognito.[1] Thus for the twenty-seven writings of the New Testament all are essentially anonymous except for perhaps nine letters of Paul and three of an unnamed but individualized elder who wrote the epistles of John. This means that roughly seven-tenths of the New Testament is anonymous or pseudonymous. But even when the actual author does not identify himself we can still distinguish between genuinely naïve composition and those writings in which consciousness of authorship transpires. Here the work of the author of Luke-Acts stands out, for while he does not name himself he does use the first person singular in introducing both parts of his work, and may refer to himself in his use of 'we' in parts of the book of Acts. In such features we find ourselves no doubt on the borderland of the Christian writings of a later period when the Fathers entered boldly into the sphere of secular literature, when anonymity

[1] Two of our letters lack the proper naming of the author at the beginning (Hebrews, I John) or other formal features of the type. Some have a very general address. In such cases we recognize either that the author is using the letter-form for wider purposes or that later editors have imposed an epistolary frame upon writings which were originally not letters. I John, however, is probably to be recognized as a genuine letter to a number of churches in a limited area.

was abandoned at the same time that the world's literary practices and forms were freely adopted.

The climate and practice of pagan composition in this period imposed conscious literary authorship and a sense of literary property. It also had its own sophisticated forms of pseudonymous writing. Students in classical schools were taught to write exercises in the name and style of famous models. Letters were published giving themselves out to be the work of famous philosophers of the past. Oracles in the Orphic, Hermetic or Sibylline traditions were fathered upon Thoth or other mythical figures.[1] Motives to this kind of pseudonymity began to overlay the older kind in the Christian literature of the second century and may well be present in the cases of the Pastoral Epistles and II Peter. Among the Christian Gnostics the influence came earlier.

When we find pseudonymous writings in the canon (on our view, for example, in Ephesians and I Peter), we are not to think that the real author sought to deceive or to acquire a specious acceptance of his writing by ascribing it to an apostle. His impulse was disingenuous and irreproachable. The unknown writer felt that he was a voice of the shared tradition and revelation, that all truth and leading was of a piece and derived from Christ and his chosen vessels. His procedure, to quote Professor Kurt Aland, was

> the logical consequence of the presupposition that the Spirit himself was the author. If it was not always through all the apostles together that the Spirit was thought to speak [as in the case of the Didache], it was through the outstanding apostles individually, through those, indeed, that were most highly reverenced at a particular time and place. In early Christianity Holy Scripture did not know any author in the modern sense. The reporter of Holy Events (Gospels and Acts) remained anonymous.[2]

Professor Aland's view so formulated does not, perhaps, meet all the circumstances. He himself recognizes that with the Pastoral Epistles we may well have an example of the transition from the earlier, more naïve type of pseudonymity to the later, more sophisticated kind. In this later period the authority of the apostles took on a more formal character. Sooner or later writings originally anonymous like Matthew, John and Hebrews were assigned apostolic

[1] F. Torm, *Die Psychologie der Pseudonymität im Hinblick auf die Literatur des Urchristentums* (Gütersloh 1932).

[2] Kurt Aland, 'The Problem of Anonymity and Pseudonymity in Christian Literature of the First Two Centuries', *JTS* 7/1 (April 1961), p. 45.

authorship, though in the case of John it is only at first intimated by appendix and interpolation. But throughout, the impulse and procedure were ingenuous and reflect an intense sense of the continuities of the apostolic household of faith. Professor Aland rightly observes that it is not anonymity or pseudonymity that calls for explanation in the Early Church but rather those cases where a real author identifies himself.

Paul's genuine letters offer us the best examples of this. Here we have evidently self-conscious authorship. How does this agree with the naïve anonymity of the early Christian rhetoric? Here we confront a main feature of the early Christian epistles which we have not yet mentioned. The letter-form in the New Testament is not a wholly novel creation as is the gospel-form. But it is nevertheless radically new in one significant respect: the form of the address and opening.[1] Here we have a Christianizing of the conventional greeting and good wishes which are regular features of ancient letters, such that both the writer Paul and those to whom he writes are drawn by thanksgiving and intercession into common awareness of the Gospel. This colours the entire letter. It also transforms the role of Paul from that of an individual letter-writer to that of an apostle under mandate, as he evokes the meaning of the word of God in the Gospel and its corollaries of instruction. Paul, as he himself says, is only a minister of the word and not a rhetorician. Thus even the signed personal letters of Paul also illustrate the new speech-phenomenon whose feature is, if not anonymity, at least a corporate transcendence of the self through the Spirit. This does not mean that what we call 'personality' or 'individuality' are denied in the new faith, but they are found in a new context according to which they are both humbled and exalted. If we press this question back to Jesus himself and ask about the relation of his personality to the authority of his words we raise a fundamental theological question. But the truth would be missed if we gave an answer in secular terms and spoke of Jesus as a creative poet or artist in language. Who Jesus was and the nature of his utterance can only be rightly understood in terms of his calling. As we read in the Gospel of John: 'My teaching is not mine, but his who sent me. . . . He who speaks on his own authority seeks his own glory; but he who seeks the glory of him who sent him is true. . . . I have not come of my own accord . . .' (7.16, 18, 28).

We have been looking at the chief literary genres of the New

[1] See Paul Schubert, *Form and Function of the Pauline Thanksgivings* (Berlin 1939).

Testament, gospel, epistle, etc., and we may well pause here to ask what we learn here about our main topic, early Christian rhetoric. They represent, indeed, a later phase, that of writing. Yet in that mode they carry on essential features of the earliest Christian utterance: its creative novelty in styles; its dramatic immediacy and dialogue feature; its use of common idiom and media; its addiction to narrative; its subordination of the personal role or talent to the Spirit in the community, especially in anonymity or pseudonymity.

v

When we first survey the literary forms and styles of an alien body of literature like that of the New Testament, or the Old, we naturally try to help ourselves by using the categories and pigeon-holes with which we are acquainted. Arrangements of the Old Testament for modern readers are familiar which use the classifications of epic for its early narratives, oratory for the prophets, drama for Job, and other terms for other parts, ballad, elegy, short story, etc. A similar approach to the New Testament suggests biography for the Gospels, history for the Book of Acts, formal epistle or treatise for the letters, and other terms for lesser forms: ode, allegory, anecdote, etc. Sometimes such modernizations are suggestive as when we call the Book of Revelation a surrealist work or a fresco, or chapters thirteen to seventeen in John a 'farewell discourse'. But such procedures are bound to mislead us. Even when we bring such basic categories into play as those of Aristotle we are moving in a different world. Just as the Gospels cannot well be classed as tragedy, so the distinctions in the New Testament poems of lyric, dramatic, epic, elegiac do not fit.

This should confirm our discovery in literary criticism today that Western aesthetic norms are often parochial. They need to be widened to make room for what non-Western arts and imagination can teach us. Modern painting, as is well known, has been renewed by contacts with South Pacific sensibility by Gauguin and others; modern sculpture by pre-Columbian art-forms of America and by other so-called primitive works; the modern drama by the Japanese tradition. In poetry fertilization both of verse itself and of criticism has come from the idioms not only of early Anglo-Saxon and Provencal poetry but also Chinese. In the light of such shocks contemporary English literary criticism has gone beyond familiar typologies, while the artists have evolved styles consonant with a global humanity that stands today on the brink of uncharted futures.

In this light a new approach is possible to the Bible as literature apart from formal theological considerations. There are, in fact, to-day literary critics like Northrop Frye and Kenneth Burke, as well as Erich Auerbach, who have dealt with the rhetoric of Scripture with this more adequate kind of humanistic resource. Similarly, students of symbolism have recognized the place of biblical language-forms in comparative studies of myth and mythical thinking that do not stop with Western examples. Our point is that our early Christian literary arts were different from those that ancient paganism produced, and that Greek and traditional humanist categories are inadequate as measuring rods.

It is true that when modern scholarship began to give particular attention to our earliest Christian writings and their styles, it naturally sought for resemblances in the pagan Greek writings that were contemporary. Great classicists like Eduard Norden and authorities on Hellenistic literature like Paul Wendland, as well as New Testament form-critics like K. L. Schmidt and Bultmann, participated in these comparative studies. The task was complicated, since the rise of Christianity was linked with Palestinian Jewish culture and the Aramaic tongue. The early oral traditions of the Church underwent also Hellenistic-Jewish influence and thus at least indirectly Hellenistic-pagan influences. But for purposes of comparison on the formal side the Christian Gospels, Epistles, and other genres were compared with pagan Greek models. This proved on the whole a blind alley. The existing Greek literary forms were almost all sophisticated and artistic. They belonged to a different world. Even much Jewish literature in Greek—Josephus, the Letter of Aristeas, etc.—was determined by a professional literary tradition and was consciously artistic and written for a wide public.

Thus the conclusion was reached that none of the New Testament writings could be identified as 'literature' as then understood in the Roman Empire. As Franz Overbeck showed, the primitive Christian writings from AD 50 to as late as 160 (that is, including the Apostolic Fathers) fall outside the history of literature properly so called. They were sub-literary products and naïve in the best sense. Except among the heretics, it is only when we come down to the apologists and especially to Clement of Alexandria that we find Christian writings which can be identified with the patterns of literary art of the Greco-Roman world. The Christian forms have to be studied for themselves. As Overbeck noted,

Gospel, Acts and Apocalypse are historical forms which at a given moment disappear in the Christian Church.'[1]

The primitive Christian literature is one which Christianity, so to speak, fashioned out of its own resources, in the sense that it grew solely out of the soil and inner interests of the Christian community before its merging with the world about it. . . . Even when it used forms available to it, it appropriated only such as were peculiar to the *religious* literature of earlier times.[2]

It is worth while dwelling upon this creative and non-literary period of Christian writings. The new speech and speech-forms of the Gospel followed the law of the Gospel and of Christ himself: humiliation and incognito. Here, too, transposing, the outsider could say, this literature

> Grew up before him like a young plant,
>   and like a root out of dry ground;
> [it] had no form or comeliness that we
>   should look at [it],
> and no beauty that we should desire [it].

Eduard Norden in his comparison of Hellenistic literature with the Christian writings notes particularly the cult of individuality and love of fame and earthly immortality associated with the former. The Roman Campagna, he writes,

has gigantic memorials with pompous inscriptions and this same Campagna covers the bones of countless Christians whose resting-places are indicated only by tablets with the simple formula, *in pace*, while their unknown names are covered by eternal night. The same contrast holds so far as literary individuality is concerned: on the one hand, *exegi monumentum*, with what follows: this is classical antiquity; on the other hand, the Christian motif: 'it will be given you what you shall speak, for it is not you who speak but the spirit of your Father that speaketh in you'.[3]

It is also interesting to observe the gradual steps by which the early Christian speech and speech-forms took over and, indeed, mastered the patterns of classical eloquence and rhetoric. This takes us beyond the period of the New Testament. The impulse to dignify the Gospels in the eyes of the cultured appears already in the case of

---

[1] Franz Overbeck, 'Über die Anfänge der patristischen Literatur', *Historische Zeitschrift* 48 (1882), p. 432. Cited by W. G. Kümmel, *Das Neue Testament* (Munich 1958), p. 356.

[2] *Ibid.*, p. 443 (Kümmel, p. 257).

[3] *Die antike Kunstprosa* II (Leipzig 1898), p. 455.

Justin Martyr in the middle of the second century. He commends them as the *apomnēmoneumata* or *memorabilia* of the apostles, the same title which Xenophon gave to his literary account of Socrates, and which was used for other pagan biographical writings. But this classification is mistaken on many counts.[1] Many Christians since Justin, including Papias, have prejudiced a right understanding of our Gospels by overzealous attempts to put them in a literary or historical class to which they do not belong and did not aspire.

In the latter part of the second century Christian writers who had been trained in the philosophical schools of the period entered the field of literature proper to defend Christianity before the Roman authorities in time of threatened persecution. But even before this the authors of our apocryphal gospels, acts, epistles, etc., wrote in secular styles. Their way of composition often betrays an inadequate understanding of the Gospel or a concession to shallow curiosities, miracle-mongering and the love of entertainment. For example, the gospels of the infancy indulge in highly coloured stories as to the birth and childhood of Jesus and of the miracles wrought by the infant Christ for which we find our best parallels in such pagan biographies as that of Hercules.[2] Sometimes more elevated but still misconceived traits appear. The now much-publicized *Gospel of Thomas* consists of one hundred and fourteen sayings ascribed to Jesus. These are often significant and often related to sayings we also know in the Gospels. But the erroneous presupposition behind it is that Jesus was chiefly significant as an oracle of profound wisdom.[3]

The apocryphal *Acts of Paul and Thecla*, like most popular pagan biographies, has a fanciful description of the physical appearance of Paul that is often quoted. But one of the characteristics of Christian literature nearer the source is that it never gives such portraiture of its personages, whether Jesus or Judas, whether Mary Magdalene or Salome.[4] Incidentally, this is one reason why those really acquainted with the early Christian sensibility have little interest in

[1] K. L. Schmidt, 'Die Stellung der Evangelien in der allgemeine Literaturgeschichte', *EYXAPIΣTHPION* II (Göttingen 1923), pp. 55–58.

[2] See Marcel Simon, *Hercule et le christianisme* (Strasbourg 1955), pp. 53, 64

[3] On the literary form of this gospel see Bertil Gärtner, *The Theology of the Gospel According to Thomas* (New York 1961), ch. II. It is true that we have other Gnostic gospels of the same or related sects which have a narrative character and that even in the Gospel of Thomas Jesus is presented as a heavenly revealer. But the aspect of revealed knowledge is common to all.

[4] Relevant here is the discussion of the Hebrew attitude to external appearances in T. Boman, *Hebrew Thought Compared with Greek*, pp. 74–122.

supposed paintings by St Luke or supposed contemporary effigies of Christ, as in the case of the Veronica. We know that the beginnings of Christian visual art are to be dated in the third century. The beginnings of Christian literary art, in the classical sense, dated perhaps one hundred years earlier.

How this came about is well stated by Eduard Norden:

> To be understood and to be effective [Christian literature] had to retain the antique forms in literature as in the plastic arts. But most significant was the fact that these forms which because of loss of substance had come to be pursued for their own sake, and like a self-sufficing ornament had lapsed into mere flourish, now were filled with new content and thus were transmitted to the human race for all time to come.[1]

In another passage Norden tellingly cites the lament of Libanios over the degradation of pagan eloquence in the time of Julian. This sophist made the profound observation that genuine eloquence and the sense of the sacred go together (*ho logos* and *ta hiera*). Libanios connected the decline of pagan rhetoric with the desecration of ancient pagan sanctities. But, adds Norden, he failed to recognize that at the very time he wrote a new world of holiness was conjoined with an incomparable new Christian eloquence in the preaching and writing of Gregory, Basil and John Chrysostom, and that thereby the survival of Latin eloquence was assured.[2]

We have stepped beyond the limits of our canon to observe how Christian speech eventually laid hold of artistic media of communication current in paganism. But every step of the way, beginning with Jesus himself, represented an identification with and a renewal of existing idioms. In one sense, as language the Gospel met each man and each people where they were—was 'all things to all men'—in another sense it spoke a new word to all.

[1] *Op. cit.*, pp. 464–5.
[2] *Ibid.*, pp. 451–2.

III

THE DIALOGUE

And I will say to Not my people, 'You are my people';
and he shall say, 'Thou art my God.'

HOSEA 2.23

BEHIND THE FAMILIAR twenty-seven writings of the New Testament we should learn to be aware of the spoken utterance on
which so much of it rests. Oral speech is where it all began.
Jesus and his first followers used the different modes of language
which we know as dialogue, story and poem, well before it occurred
to anyone to set anything down on papyrus or leather or tablet. Even
when they did come to write we can overhear the living voices,
speaking and praising. This kind of writing is very close to speech.
Again we can see one reason why the literature of the primitive
Church was not literature in the classic or artistic sense. Artistic
writing is by definition at a second remove from native speech and
has taken on a further degree of conventionality.

The roots of the Old Testament were in oral recital and chant
and the transmission of these long depended on memory alone. We
have noted that Jesus did not write and that Paul only wrote under
constraint and with reluctance. Even when the Gospels had long been
in existence the Church Fathers frequently cited the words and deeds
of Christ not from these writings but from the still growing oral
tradition, often in a somewhat different version. Papias about AD 140
illuminates this procedure when he says, 'I did not suppose that
information from books would help me so much as the word of a
living and surviving voice.'[1] Even in the third century we find
Origen reluctant to write. He prefers oral instruction, face to face
with his students and congregations. In his view the Gospel as the
Word of God is properly addressed to the ear and not written for
the eye. As Franz Overbeck observed, the Church Fathers are, for the

[1] Eusebius, *H. E.* III, 39.4 (Loeb I, p. 293).

most part, 'writers who do not want to be such'. Yet circumstances imposed writing. Augustine explicitly justifies the idea of a Christian *rhetor* and a Christian rhetoric,[1] in written as well as spoken eloquence, by appeal to Scripture itself.

We turn in this chapter to one of the basic speech-modes of the Early Church, that of the dialogue. Here evidently we have to do with a basic oral phenomenon and a very human one, that of conversation. It is appropriate therefore to look again into this whole matter of oral versus written discourse in the beginnings of Christianity.

I

It is curious to remark the hesitations exhibited toward writing in much religion and poetry. This preference for oral rather than written discourse is prominent in Judaism and Christianity in the period with which we are concerned. The interpretations of the Torah by the scribes could only be transmitted orally in this period, as is well known, despite the great burden on the memory of teacher and pupil. In the Christian Church, except for letters, the writing stage was slow in coming and even when written gospels were in existence, oral tradition was still for a long time very significant and even preferred.

There were, no doubt, special factors present in the disinclination toward writing on the part of Jews and Christians in this time. In primitive societies the first introduction of the art of writing always encounters resistance. But writing was, of course, not a revolutionary new procedure for either Jews or Christians who possessed the written law and various other cherished texts. Yet the Pharisees insisted that oral law should remain oral. Why? Probably because they continued to respect a long-established usage. To quote Birger Gerhardsson:

> The Pharisees thus stand out in the struggle with the Sadducees . . . as energetic advocates of the principle that oral Torah is, and must remain, *oral* Torah. It is probable that the Pharisees are here conserving a more ancient practice. It is in fact likely that in the third and second centuries BC, writing had still not come into such widespread use in the non-priestly circles from which the Pharisaic scholars came, as it was to do in the Hellenized priestly circles in Jerusalem.[2]

[1] See Lukas Vischer, 'Die Rechtfertigung der Schriftstellerei in der alten Kirche', *TZ* 12/3 (Mai-Juni 1956), p. 329.
[2] Gerhardsson, *op. cit.*, pp. 25, 158. To this motive Gerhardsson adds that of a rejection of the Sadducaic practice of notation; the impulse to restrict the circle of those who would have access to this private material; and possibly the high reverence felt now for the sacred written Torah by contrast.

Among the first Christians, different factors operated. That Jesus did not write is connected as we have seen with his mission. Immediacy was of the essence in his challenge and dialogue. If for some time his followers did not write, it was not because they followed scribal custom. It was again, as in the case of Jesus, because the Gospel represented a new and living speech. For this dynamic and prophetic word the conventionality of writing was inappropriate. The Word must not be bound. Here it is relevant to remind ourselves of the considerations which have been adduced to explain the taboos on writing which appear in early societies. To quote Gerhardsson again:

> We are familiar with the opposition to letters and writing which manifested itself in many cultures at the time when the art of writing was introduced and which lives on, in various ways and forms, long afterward. . . . Such unwillingness may occasionally be more in the nature of superstition: we know that writing was originally a magical process. Sometimes it may be of a more rational nature: doubt is expressed as to the ability of letters and written words to reproduce the full life, power and meaning of the spoken word. This latter form was by no means the least common expression of opposition to the written word in the ancient Near East and in Classical Antiquity.[1]

The fact is, the unique speech-event of the Gospel was of such a character that here again, as in so-called primitive societies, the power of oral speech necessarily excluded the conventionality of writing. Perhaps we should say that the fundamental matter is not the distinction between oral and written, but between personal and impersonal, between first-hand and second-hand. In the early days of the Gospel this distinction required the oral mode. Later on when writing became necessary the writing was still personal and first-hand.

We seek now, however, to uncover the older deposits of early Christian speech behind the New Testament writings. These writings have their peculiar shapes. But so had the earlier oral utterance. All human gestures including the gesture of speech have their patterns, as has, indeed, the song of birds. Communication of any kind is subject to the law of form. The earliest myth and ritual of mankind always has had its rhythm and symmetry. In this sense there is already formal pattern at the very origins of the new utterance of the Gospel.

There is a mysterious combination of novelty and tradition in the

[1] *Ibid.*, p. 157.

sayings of Jesus and in the oldest confessions or recitations of the Church. Long before Jesus, not only in Israel but in the ancient Near East, a high prestige had been assigned to the arts of felicitous speech. In the Egypt of the Pharaohs rhetorical accomplishment was cherished as more difficult than any other activity, and credited to the God Thoth. In the Old Testament David was praised as 'apt in speech' as well as 'skilful in playing' (I Sam. 16.18), and Solomon became the type of those who were honoured for their pungent sayings, proverbs and riddles. The perennial features of natural eloquence had been developed to a high art in the tradition that lay behind the parables and aphorisms of Jesus. Corresponding antecedents existed for early Christian prayers and canticles. But here again we find something not only old but new.

We have already named three particular speech-forms that appear in the oldest period of the Gospel, predestined patterns, as it were, which renew themselves throughout the whole New Testament period. These are: the dialogue, the story, and the poem. The word of God found its appropriate vehicles both in the sense of images and of forms. Within limits one can say that to this very day and always Christianity will most characteristically communicate itself at least in these three modes: the drama, the narrative, the poem—just as it will always be bound in some degree to its primordial symbols, no matter how much the world may change. In a double sense Father Thornton's statement holds true: 'The contents of the revelation are mysteriously inseparable from the forms in which they are conveyed.'[1]

In the chapters that follow we shall therefore extend our examination of the New Testament literary forms. It is now to parts of the writings, indeed often brief parts, that we give our attention. We turn first to the dialogue.

II

Dialogue, address and response, question and answer, certainly represent a fundamental speech-situation and rhetorical form. Language in the nature of the case implies a hearer. Two-way communication is only the extension to the human level of the organic interrelation of nature and has its vocal antecedents in the signals of birds and beasts. Speech means speech to. . . . Even the act of naming or giving a new name in primitive societies has overtones of

[1] *The Common Life in the Body of Christ* (London 1942), p. 3.

mutuality. For address anticipates reply. It is, therefore, not surprising that dialogue appears as an elemental form in many cultural expressions. Folklore, fairy tales and saga evidence this lively dramatic phenomenon. Here is encounter. Here human nature comes to life. Here we see the perennial love of a clever reply or retort. Here we find the basis of the wide use of direct discourse, a feature that is markedly characteristic of the oral tradition both of the Old and the New Testaments.

In more formal rhetoric we find the same interpersonal encounter reflected in various literary genres: the Platonic dialogue, the ancient diatribe, the imaginary conversation, poems written with answering refrains or in the two-voices mode, and of course in drama.

The character of religion as it appears in both Old and New Testament makes the dialogue an inevitable form of rhetorical expression. God is known as one who speaks, addresses, calls, initiates agreements or covenants, engages in public trial-scenes, as well as one who invites to mutual converse and understanding. It is he who says, 'Come now, let us reason together' (Isa. 1.18), or, 'Son of man, stand upon your feet, and I will speak with you' (Ezek. 2.1). The Bible is therefore full of dialogue and of a most searching kind. And it is not only a dialogue between God and man. For where man is so defined it follows that the mutual relation of man and man is charged with significance. The Psalmist can say of a friend who, indeed, later betrayed him: 'We took sweet counsel together' (55.14).

The implicit dialogue in all biblical religion comes to rhetorical expression in the Old Testament in striking ways. We naturally think first of the primordial interchanges between God and Adam and Eve, between God and Cain; the covenant-agreements with the patriarchs and Moses; the great colloquies of the Book of Job. There are passages in the Psalms where the common worshipper is overheard in silent converse with God, it may be in expostulation and pleading on his bed in the night watches. We have also the dramatic court-scenes in which God and Israel occupy the changing roles of plaintiff and accused. In the forty-first chapter of Isaiah, indeed, God convokes all the nations of the earth to be witnesses to the validity of his case:

> Listen to me in silence, O coastlands;
>   let the peoples renew their strength;
> let them approach, then let them speak;
>   let us draw near for judgment (41.1).

As with the dialogue between God and man, so with that between his messengers and their hearers. The style of the Bible often bears witness to the rejoinders, protests, even blasphemies of the human interlocutors. Hans Walter Wolff observes that the Book of Hosea is made up of reports by the prophet's disciples, who 'preserved his words soon after each discussion with his hearers'. The words of Hosea as transmitted to us still convey the opposition and self-justification of those addressed by the prophet, and sometimes their very words.

> These sketches usually still radiate the heat of excited discussion; the sayings are not declaimed in the style of a sermon but are formulated in terms of a lively conversation, just as certainly as they originated in the loneliness of the prophet with his God. Only seldom are they clothed in forms of cultic order, (as in the repentance Psalm with its answer of consolation in 6.1–3, 4 f., and 14.1–3, 4 ff.): as a rule they correspond to the alternating forms of speech which have their home in the legal assemblies of the clans or the local community before the elders in the gate.[1]

This dialogue-form, after all, takes us to the heart of biblical religion, namely prayer itself. The new speech-freedom of the Gospel was associated with a new sense of the person, human and divine. It is not surprising again, therefore, that we find omnipresent and novel dialogue forms both as between man and man and man and God.

One bridge to our New Testament examples is found in the antiphonal recitation of Jewish temple worship. This became prominent after the exile, reflecting the greater participation of the people in the cultus.

> The community shared in the singing of the Psalms by the temple singers as they offered responses with Amen, Hallelujah or with longer refrains (I Chron. 16.41). The doxologies at the ends of the main sections of the Psalter have a similar significance. This led to the wider popular use of the Psalms and so to their enormous influences on the liturgies and piety of all time.[2]

Since the use of the Psalms has always had antiphonal aspects this observation is of special interest to our present concern.

[1] 'Guilt and Salvation: A Study of the Prophecy of Hosea', *Interpretation* 15/3 (July 1961), p. 275.
[2] I. Elbogen, *Der jüdische Gottesdienst* (Frankfurt-am-Main 1924), p. 237.

III

The New Testament is full of voices speaking and replying. In the Synoptic Gospels this dialogue pattern appears especially in the many little vignettes in which we hear Jesus questioning or questioned, and in the parables of Jesus in which vivid colloquy in direct discourse often occurs.[1] Implicit dialogue also appears in those occasions where a fateful naming or calling goes forth from God himself or from Christ, as when Jesus is identified as the Son at his baptism, or when Jesus himself addresses Peter as the Rock, or indeed, when he addresses Jerusalem in lament for its refusal to respond. In the Fourth Gospel we recognize a recurrent pattern of conversation between Christ and his antagonists or his disciples, in this case peculiar since so often the questions addressed to Christ have so evidently an obtuse character. Thus, indeed, the disparity of the world and God's truth is dramatized.

In Paul's letters we are taught to recognize the familiar Hellenistic *diatribe* style, according to which the writer simulates objectors and inquirers and answers them. In the Book of Revelation we come upon whole series of interchanges in direct discourse, as though in a transcendental drama. We hear voices of angels, voices of elders, voices of beasts, voices of multitudes and trumpet voices. This work in other respects maximizes the auditory as well as the visionary sense. As compared with the Jewish apocalypses it is less a literary composition than a mimetic recital or oratorio. We find recurrent dialogue elements often having a liturgical character or climax. For example, in the seventh chapter:

An elder:	Who are these clothed in white robes, and whence have they come?
The seer:	Sir, you know.
An elder:	These are they who have come out of the great tribulation . . . (vv. 13–14).

And the reply passes over into a recitative of words of ancient prophecy and psalmody.

We can point to other antiphonal elements in the New Testament, especially in connection with liturgical practices like baptism where the question of the baptizer and the reply of the initiate are already

---

[1] Thus in the parable of the talents in Matt. 25 each of the three servants reports in direct discourse to the master as to his disposition of the entrusted funds, and to each the master replies: 'Well done, good and faithful servant'; 'You wicked and slothful servant'; etc.

emerging.[1] For an example we can cite the account in Acts of
Philip's baptism of the Ethiopian eunuch, Acts 8.37, margin. Here
the later church baptismal dialogue has imposed itself upon the
Western text. In this text and in Irenaeus we get the following
colloquy before the act of baptism (the MSS gives slightly different
wordings):

The eunuch:	See, here is water! What is to prevent my being baptized?
Philip:	If you believe with all your heart, you may.
The eunuch:	I believe that Jesus Christ is the Son of God.

The challenge and reply of the faithful when brought to trial is
also reflected in many passages where the confession of Christ by the
Spirit is set against the summons to deny him; each one a paradigm
of the dialogue of the Christian and the world.[2] To these should be
added debate-situations where scorn or defamation is met with the
true witness, or where the ultimate lie or blasphemy is set against the
voice of truth:

> If we say, 'We have fellowship with him'
>   while we walk in darkness,
> we lie and do not live according to the truth. . . .
>
> If we say, 'we have no sin,'
> we deceive ourselves, and the truth is not in us. . . .
>
> If we say, 'we have not sinned'
> we make him a liar and his word is not
>   in us. (I John 1.6–10.)

Of course, dialogue can be found in all literature and in all
scriptures. It is human to delight in a shrewd reply or a dramatic
give-and-take, just as it is human to tell a good story. It is a question,
however, of depth. Take one example from the fourteenth chapter of
Mark: Peter denying Christ in the courtyard while Jesus is being
tried. One of the maids of the high priest presses Peter:

> You also were with the Nazarene, Jesus.
> Peter denies it, saying,
>   I neither know nor understand what you mean.

[1] In the Jewish ritual of the Passover the *pater familias* traditionally answered
questions put to him as to the meaning of the various features of the meal. Jesus'
interpretation of the bread and the wine may be seen against such a background,
even though originally the Last Supper may not have been a Passover observance.

[2] Cf. Matt. 10.17–20; Acts 4.5–22; 5.27–42; 6.9–8.1, and trial scenes involving
Paul, Acts 22.30–23.10; 24.2–25; 25.23–26.32.

After another similar challenge one of the bystanders says,
Certainly you are one of them; for you are a Galilean.
And then Peter, invoking a curse on himself and by oath replies,
I do not know this man of whom you speak.

This is the very anecdote that Erich Auerbach cites in his *Mimesis* to illustrate the abysmal realism of the early Christian literature and its styles. We have here a plebeian, low-life episode involving personages that are nonentities—a police-court disturbance. Yet in our gospel context all the issues of world-history gather about it; issues of blessedness and damnation, whether for Peter, or for those to whom the early message was orally preached, or for us who read it after two millennia. This new plain rhetoric of the Gospel was what it was only because it was prompted by a new direct speech or word of God himself to men. What makes such stories and such dialogue so formidable is that in each one God, as it were, forces us to give him a face-to-face answer, or, to look him in the eye.

To return to the Gospel of John, we have noted that dialogue here between Jesus and his hearers is often based upon somewhat inept questions. Jesus says that one must be born anew and Nicodemus asks how one can be born when he is old. 'Can he enter a second time into his mother's womb and be born?' (3.3–4). Jesus says to the woman of Samaria that he would have given her living water, and she asks where he would get it, since the well is deep and he has nothing to draw with (4.10–11). When Jesus speaks of giving himself as the bread of life, the disputants say, 'How can this man give us his flesh to eat?' (6.51–52). In Jesus' farewell discourse, after his washing of the disciples' feet, we have a good illustration of how this Gospel enlivens the teaching of Jesus by punctuating it with their expressions of surprise and misunderstanding.[1] Peter asks, 'Lord, we do not know where you are going; how can we know the way?' (14.5). Philip prays, 'Lord, show us the Father, and we shall be satisfied' (14.8). Judas asks, 'Lord, how is it that you will manifest yourself to us, and not to the world?' (14.22). In all such interchanges in John we have somewhat staged dialogue, and the same could be said of certain later editorial elements in the Synoptic Gospels.[2]

[1] Bertil Gärtner, *The Theology of the Gospel According to Thomas* (New York 1961), p. 26.
[2] Especially those bearing on the 'Messianic secret' and the true understanding of the parables or the miracles of the loaves; cf. Mark 4.10–20; 7.17–23; 8.14–21; 9.9–13. For a discussion bearing on the Synoptic Gospels as well as John see C. H. Dodd, 'The Dialogue Form in the Gospels', *Bulletin of the John Rylands Library* 37/1 (September, 1954).

For this procedure in John we have good analogies in Gnostic literature and now especially in the new Coptic texts discovered in Upper Egypt in 1946. In these the risen Christ is presented as the revealer of secret wisdom to certain favoured disciples or women, and his disclosures are often made in dialogue or conversation scenes. In fact, the dialogue form has been artificially constructed to place the Gnostic teaching in Jesus' own mouth and thus make it more striking.[1] As Gärtner writes:

> There is thus no doubt that the question-and-answer form occupies a key position in Gnostic literature. The style is often extremely naïve: the questions are artificial, and exist only to allow the Gnostic 're-vealer' to share his teachings on the position of Christ in the world-all, or the ascent of the soul to the world of light.[2]

In such material there is evidently an artistic impulse at work which dramatizes Jesus as an oracle in face-to-face encounter with man's ignorance, drowsiness or intoxication. In the now famous Gospel of Thomas with its many pronouncements usually intro-duced by the words, 'Jesus said', or 'He said', the dialogue feature occasionally appears. Thus:

> His disciples said to Him:
> When will the repose of the dead come about
> and when will the new world come?
> He said to them:
> What you expect has come,
> but you know it not.[3]

Here as in the Gnostic dialogue generally the emphasis falls on Jesus as one who answers questions about mysteries. The difference between such encounters and those in the Gospels is significant. It is partly a matter of theme: as Paul says, love is better than all mysteries and all knowledge. But it is more profoundly a matter of personal involvement. The dialogue in the Gospels is directed to the heart rather than to some faculty in us of higher knowledge.

In the case of the Gospel of John we have an exception which proves the rule. Much of Jesus' teaching here is framed in the form

---

[1] Gärtner, op. cit., pp. 23–24.

[2] P. 24. Note his example of how truths stated in the letter-form (in the *Letter of Eugnostos*) are re-edited in a dialogue-form (by the author of *Jesu Christi Sophia*), pp. 24–25.

[3] Saying no. 51; trans. *The Gospel According to Thomas*, Coptic Text Established and Translated by A. Guillaumont, H.-Ch. Puech, G. Quispel, W. Till and Yassah 'abd al Masīḥ (New York 1959), p. 29.

of artistic conversation or dialogue, and as we have seen it resembles at first sight the Gnostic models. It also concerns itself with their topics such as knowing the truth and the difference between light and darkness. But the answer to Nicodemus focuses in John 3.16, 'God so loved the world that he gave his only Son.' The conversation with the woman of Samaria exposes her moral situation. The disclosures offered by Jesus in his farewell discourses to the Twelve carry with them the new commandment, 'that you love one another as I have loved you'. Thus the author of the Fourth Gospel in this feature of dialogue as in other respects indeed uses Gnostic language and styles, but radically converts these to his own Christian purposes.

The English philosopher, Ian T. Ramsey, has a section on what he calls the 'many conversations at cross purposes' that occur in this Gospel. In his book, *Religious Language*[1] he argues that religious revelation inevitably calls for unusual or, as he says, 'odd' style and expression. In John he observes that 'right from the start' its language is 'much more improper' than that of Mark, for example. He then takes up the episode of the woman of Samaria in chapter four. At first, he notes, there is a quite natural interchange between her and Jesus about getting a drink of water and about the dealings of Jews and Samaritans, then the dialogue shifts. To quote Ramsey,

> At this point Jesus shoots into the situation another language altogether . . . 'Go call thy husband.' Here is a shock; the light begins to break; the situation begins to come alive.

Finally we reach Jesus' mysterious self-identification as Messiah, or rather his use of the God-formula, 'I am'. And Ramsey concludes:

> Only then does the light break, eyes are opened, and there is a Christian disclosure. Once again we see that a Gospel-situation is one for whose expression language must be used with logical impropriety.[2]

What he means is that the *Ego eimi* formula here is syntactically shocking, just as is Jesus' statement at another point in this Gospel: 'Before Abraham was, I am.'

Thus we may find in the dialogue between heaven and earth that occurs in the New Testament elements of distortion, or hyperbole and incomprehension. We shall find an analogy to this in the traits of the extraordinary that Jesus introduces into the otherwise lifelike circumstances of his parables. We are reminded of Paul Tillich's

[1] London 1957.
[2] Pp. 124–5.

thesis that in the arts it is the feature of distortion, perhaps only slight, which is the sign of genuine religious immediacy and creativeness.

IV

What elements are there in the New Testament that could come under the head of dramatic literature? Certainly this omnipresence of dialogue points that way. It is true that neither the Old Testament or the New includes any technically dramatic genres as the Greeks knew them or as we understand them. Even the Book of Job is only called a drama by poetic licence, since there is so little action in it. In his *Anatomy of Criticism*, Northrop Frye remarks that 'the Book of Job is clearly an imaginative drama, but the Book of Job is more important, and closer to Christ's practise of revelation through parable'.[1] The Song of Solomon probably comes closest to the play-form, since it represents a kind of libretto for the successive acts of a wedding and wedding feast. The really conspicuous drama of Israel and its later Jewish social life revolved about the Temple and the ritual actions of the great feasts. For these the Psalter offers us evidence enough of the processions, entrances, incantations, postures, responses, musical aspects and crowning sacrifical actions of the priests and the people, and their dialogue with God. Indeed, the deeper mythology of the feasts recalled the ancient archetypal acts of Yahweh for his people, and the ceremonies provided annual re-enactments of the creation of the world.

But we may invoke the category of the dramatic in dealing with dialogue in the New Testament. Formally, drama means the art of the play or stage-action. But a play of any consequence rests usually upon a momentous transaction or encounter of some kind. In this sense many aspects of the style and discourse of the New Testament are dramatic, and provide material for the theatre-arts, as the whole history of Western drama shows. The Old Testament is dramatic in the sense that it records graphically the encounter and dialogue of God with men in relation to concrete historical scenes and actions. The New Testament literature and the Christian religion itself partake of this dramatic substance. Indeed, here the encounter is seen at the point of crisis, and denouement. We are in Act v. It is not surprising that the rhetoric of the first believers reflects this dynamic situation. In such an apocalyptic moment all the arts take on new forms.

[1] *Anatomy of Criticism: Four Essays* (Princeton 1957), p. 325.

We find a telling illustration in the words of a contemporary French poet, Pierre Emmanuel. A fellow poet asked him what the artist can do today in a world 'where all the laws of equilibrium are in question'. 'Why yes,' said Emmanuel. 'Since the earth quakes, the most heroic thing that the artist can do is to dance.'[1] Or, as Pere Régamey writes, in our world-crisis the arts are '*seismographes affolés*', that is, 'frenzied seismographs' of the time.[2] Certainly the character of the Book of Revelation exhibits this kind of response of language. Yet it has its own kind of order, as has the dance.

It is not only in the voices of the Apocalypse that we find early Christian dialogue characterized by dynamic stress and distinctive style. Many of the early rhetorical forms reflect these. The power that animated the early Christian movement inevitably set up high-tension relationships and conflicts in the world. In this sense the Christian consciousness only carries farther man's awareness of the mysterious powers and indeed violence that operate everywhere. W. MacNeile Dixon provides a non-theological statement of this realism in his book, *The Human Situation*:

> Nature . . . is implacable and restless and countenances no calm, no stagnation throughout her whole vast estate. If we are to understand matters aright we must think in terms of convulsions. . . . To get the scale of cosmic things we must perceive nature for what she is, as everlastingly and furiously dynamic . . . Life is a perilous adventure.[3]

The language and arts of the Gospel should always match these realities.

In this wider sense of dramatic we could point to many features of the New Testament consciousness, all reflected in its rhetoric and not least in its dialogues: signs and wonders, visions and revelations, manifestations of evil and anarchy on the one hand, of grace and beatitude on the other, celestial disturbances, cosmic and mundane warfare, images from the amphitheatre, the circus, the court and the stadium. Corresponding to this dramatic consciousness we find appropriate rhetorical features: not only potent images and tropes, paradox and hyperbole, but dialogue natural and supernatural, voices and proclamations, summons and invitations, accusations and acquittals, blessings and cursings, anathemas and doxologies, oracles

---

[1] Cited by P.-R. Régamey, *Art sacré au XXᵉsiècle* (Paris 1952), p. 25.
[2] *Ibid.*, p. 10.
[3] Pp. 49, 50.

and chants, hymns and psalms and spiritual songs. The New Testament in this respect, like Dante's *Divine Comedy*, offers us a universe of personal beings earthly and spiritual in the presence of each other and God. It is not surprising that dramatic speech in innumerable forms and modes come to our attention.

We return to actual dialogue forms as we find them in the New Testament and restrict ourselves here to the Synoptic Gospels. Among the most ancient anecdotes about Jesus which the form-critics have identified are those in which we find an exchange between him and some other person. There are, indeed, some in which the interest attaches to a clarification of Jesus' teaching or of some point of later church practice, and these are often secondary. But 'we are interested in those in which radical personal challenge and encounter are primary. The oral tradition passed these on from the beginning, because in each the later hearer or reader could see himself directly involved, and even identified, with Jesus' interlocutor. The issues in these confrontations are fundamental to the new message and way. Life or death, weal or woe, hang upon the response. There is therefore drama in these little vignettes. The exchange may be between Jesus and a disciple, a total stranger, a hostile or friendly scribe, even a demoniac. Jesus may be the questioner or it may be the other way round. The occasion may be, on Jesus' part, a call to discipleship, a testing question put to the Twelve or to the scribes, or to the Simon in whose house Jesus sat at meat; or an observation made by Jesus on the difficulty of a rich man entering the kingdom, or on the fate of the Temple; or a prediction to Peter of the betrayal or a warning against the leaven of the Pharisees. Sometimes Jesus' initial question receives no express answer and this is significant, as when he says to Judas, 'Judas, would you betray the Son of man with a kiss?' (Luke 22.48). But each hearer or reader afterwards answers this in his own heart.

On the other hand, the dialogue may be initiated by a question or a remark made *to* Jesus, and this is most often the case. There are those who propose to follow him. The disciples ask about places of honour, about how often they should forgive, about a stranger who also exorcizes. Some one intercedes for healing for himself or another, or asks that Jesus divide an inheritance. The scribes ask which commandment is the first of all; the Herodians ask about tribute; the Sadducees about the resurrection. But the basic formula is: 'What shall I do to inherit eternal life?'—in effect, 'Speak, Lord, for thy servant heareth.' Our point is that the personal dramatic character of the Gospel itself necessarily involves confrontation, not instruction in the ordinary sense but the living encounter of heart and heart, voice and voice, and that this has inevitably registered itself in the ongoing story of the Christ and in the style of the New Testament. As we have observed, it is as though God says to men one by one: 'Look me in the eye.' Jesus' message and call therefore presuppose response, not mere memorization and transcription. Through the Good News God himself by plea and invitation invites to colloquy. We are all invited by name to the banquet, that is, to the symposium. The early speech-forms made much of the dialogue involving Christ, because each follower thus found himself not only within the reach of the sound of Jesus' voice but in fateful give and take with him. Thus to this day dialectical forms are native to the Church: forms like our responses in baptism, confirmation, ordination and cate-chism; antiphonal forms in prayer, litany and reading of the Psalter; the dramatic mode in the sermon, and in the morality play, miracle play, Christmas pageant and all forms of religious drama. In all such ways taught by Scripture, we keep alive the *viva voce* encounter with God and with Christ, and anticipate the communion of the saints.

IV

THE STORY

Truth can never be told so as to be understood and not
be believed.

WILLIAM BLAKE

W E TURN NOW from the dialogue to the story. We are again
looking behind our completed Gospels and other New
Testament writings to older strata, behind our written
Scriptures to the earlier oral stages. We have seen that the movement
that began with Jesus took hold of certain primal modes of human
speech and vitalized them, and among others, the story. And here
again there was a special reason for this lying in the very genius of
the Christian revelation. The very nature of God as Judaism and
Christianity understand it comes to expression in a story as it does in
dialogue and in drama.

I

It is worth noting that, even when written, a story like a dialogue
is not far removed from oral communication, from living speech. It
is also a form that lends itself to wide popular diffusion. It is easier
to remember a story than a homily or a moral table, or even a poem.
The rabbis and the early Christian teachers were evidently aware of
this. The rabbis had various ways of formulating their teaching so
that it could be more easily remembered, just as our modern radio
advertisers have.[1] One way, of course, was to present it in poetic

[1] B. Gerhardsson, speaking of the memorization practised by the rabbis, writes:
'A great part of the haggadic material had an advantage, as compared with the
halakic; the haggadic material remained in the memory much more easily, on
account of the nature of its contents, often dramatic-epic in character, and its
poetic-didactic form. The poetic-didactic refinements (assonance, *paranomasia*,
parallelismus membrorum, etc.) of the non-halakic material in the Old Testament and
in rabbinic literature have often been remarked upon, and rightly so. . . . Haggadic
doctrinal passages (parables, narrative traditions, etc.) are often very sym-
metrically constructed; this facilitated their reconstruction in the memory if only
the beginning—or catch-word—were clear' (p. 147).

rhythm and to encourage cantillation.[1] Another way was to say it
with a story, either in a parable or by putting it in an anecdotal
context.

Jesus himself, in our view, did not deliberately shape his sayings
to the end of memorization and did not use the story-form in his
parables for this express purpose. But he did tell stories and with such
felicity that they could not be forgotten. Later his followers, like the
rabbis, cultivated devices to aid memory, and among these, anecdote
and story. Moreover, when we picture to ourselves the early Christian narrators we should make full allowance for animated and expressive narration. In ancient times even when one read to oneself
from a book, one always read aloud. Oral speech also was less in-
hibited than today. It is suggestive that in teaching the rabbis besides
using cantillation also used 'didactic facial expressions', as well as
'gestures and bodily movements to impart dramatic shape to the
doctrinal material'.[2] When we think of the early church meetings
and testimonies and narrations we are probably well guided if we
think of the way in which Vachel Lindsay read or of the appropriate
readings of James Weldon Johnson's *God's Trombones*.

Of course, in many religions we find much use of the narrative
mode: stories, myths, legends, saga. Most religious literatures similarly are like the Bible in having a considerable place for dialogues,
poems and oracles. It is a question, however, of how large and important a place each particular rhetorical form had and its character.
The narrative mode is uniquely important in Christianity. Indeed,
if one looks at other religious and philosophical classics the story
aspects may be relatively marginal. Their sacred books may often
rather take the form of philosophical instruction or mystical treatise
or didactic code or oracular vision. Even when saga and story do
come into such scriptures, the acid test remains: What view of man
and the gods do they convey? What kind of realism do they represent?

A Christian can confess his faith wherever he is, and without his
Bible, just by telling a story or a series of stories. It is through the
Christian story that God speaks, and all heaven and earth come into
it. God is an active and purposeful God and his action with and for
men has a beginning, a middle and an end like any good story. The
life of a Christian is not like a dream shot through with visions and

[1] Cf. *ibid.*, pp. 166 f.
[2] Gerhardsson, *op. cit.*, p. 168.

illuminations, but a pilgrimage, a race, in short, a history. The new Christian speech inevitably took the form of a story. The believers wanted to tell the world the way of the world as they saw it.

Moreover, in the larger history there were smaller histories. For the way of the world involved many individuals. The plot of the world-drama has included many minor as well as major roles. Episodes involving any of these could be worth the telling, as is still the case today. There are many minor characters in the Christian history. We have already cited the maid in the courtyard of the high priest. We may also think of Simon of Cyrene, who bore the Cross of Jesus, or of Paul's sister's son at the time of Paul's detention in the castle above the Temple. The anecdotes about each such individual and many more have their significance in the fact that they are related to the total world-story from alpha to omega. And such lesser histories in all their variety have their importance for us, since we recognize that those who are involved are really ourselves, Tom, Dick and Harry, along with Peter, John and Thomas. Perhaps the special character of the stories in the New Testament lies in the fact that they are not told for themselves, that they are not only about other people, but that they are always about us. They locate us in the very midst of the great story and plot of all time and space, and therefore relate us to the great dramatist and storyteller, God himself.

If we recognize our own stories in this or that New Testament story, ourselves in this or that character, it is not just a question of repetition. All the characters of God's family are different and all their infinitely various histories in time and place are different. Can one telescope the plots of all men's lives into the one plot of *Everyman*? Does Christian in *Pilgrim's Progress* stand for all of us? This question of identification arises with every story we read, whether folk-story, epic or modern novel. We identify with the hero or the villain, in their actions or in their fortunes. To take some of T. S. Eliot's characters: we are ghosts and famished with Prufrock; we are tempted with Becket; we come to understand ourselves in the web of family nemesis with Harry (*The Family Reunion*); we welcome the purging Furies with Harry, again; we resign ourselves to the long-term purification of Edward and Livinia in the common life, or some with Celia may seek the heroic way (*The Cocktail Party*); we apprehend sometimes with the speaker of the *Four Quartets* 'the intersection of the timeless moment'.

All such histories, whether from biography or fiction, may coincide in certain respects with our own history. But we do not have real repetition. The *dramatis personae* of the world's action are all different and not just so many masks of one being, one Adam, or one Ulysses or one Finnegan. There are religions and there are philosophies according to which one self or one man or one God manifests himself in myriad masks or illusions. It is not this way in the Bible. I may deny Christ with Judas, and know his pangs, but I am not Judas. I may sin with Everyman or with Faust and in the same way, but I am not Everyman or Faust. Mussolini may see himself in the role of Julius Caesar, but he is not Julius Caesar. Our pilgrim forefathers may have seen themselves as Israel crossing the Red Sea and possessing the Promised Land and fighting the Amalekites, the Hivites and the Jebusites, but there was no repetition in fact. The myriads of men taught by the Bible know that the children of God in his family are all different, and each has his own history, and his own gifts, and his own guilt and his own blessing. Nevertheless our various plots and histories overlap in various wonderful ways, and especially perhaps our moral histories. Therefore we can see ourselves in the stories of Adam, Noah, Abraham, Moses, David, etc.; or in the persons of this or that disciple of Christ or this or that person confronting his death or Resurrection, not to mention Christians of later times or the figures in the *Divine Comedy*, or *Paradise Lost*. That which makes the peculiar mystery of the life of the Christian is that the world plot plays itself over in him, yet in such a way that it is always unprecedented; that, as Paul says, 'It is not I that live but Christ liveth in me', yet as he goes on to say, 'The life that I life, I live by the faith of him that gave himself for me.'

All this means that the world is, indeed, seen by the Christian as a history and a plot, but that there are also a myriad of lesser histories within the main plot, and these sub-plots and sub-histories are real. Therefore the Scripture of Christianity is largely made up of narrative.

II

Let us look at the New Testament and make a preliminary canvass of the amount and kinds of narratives we find in it. Of course, we must include the four Gospels and the Book of Acts here. But the Gospels themselves are made up to a considerable extent of short anecdotes or stories, often very loosely linked with each other. Indeed, many of these represent little Gospels in the larger one. So one can speak of the single farthing of the Gospel (i.e. the widow's mite) as the key to salvation.[1] Furthermore, in the sayings of Jesus the parables usually take on narrative form and again some of the parables present the larger story in microcosm. Sometimes one is tempted to think that there is only one story in the world summed up in the formula of 'lost and found', and that all the stories long and short in the New Testament or the Bible itself are variations on this theme.

In the Book of Acts, again, we have many individual narratives that must likewise have been told and retold before they were strung together in the way that we now have them. In Acts also there are the numerous sermons that have a narrative character, recalling the acts of God in the past and their recent culmination. Even when Peter or Stephen or Paul are on trial, their defences have this retrospective narrative character. The Epistle to the Hebrews in its own way evokes the story of the wilderness wanderings and provides a roll-call of the heroes of faith. Some of the Epistles touch on legends of the holy figures of the past that we otherwise know of only from apocryphal sources. Certainly the Book of Revelation tells a story of cosmic catastrophes and deliverances. The symbolism of the scroll with seven seals suggests that the annals and chronicles of the world from alpha to omega are an enigma, and the key to their understanding is found in Christ alone, as though the story of the Lamb who was slain was the epitome of the whole.

Finally, there is one other important narrative element, especially in the New Testament epistles: quotations and fragments of very early confessions and hymns. Here we can see the individual Christian evangelist in his witness, or the community gathered for a baptism or for the Lord's Supper, reciting the story of salvation. When the Christian in any time or place confesses his faith, his confession turns into a narrative. When the Christian observes Christmas or Easter, in either case it is with reference to a story of things that happened.

We can make one general remark about the narrative-mode of much of the New Testament. These stories, long or short, in one way or another carry over into the future. The rounding off is usually in some sense still to come. The hearer or reader finds himself in the middle of the action. We are in the middle of the play, if not in Act v. Now, this is certainly true of the Bible epic as a whole. God's

[1] W. F. Lynch, *Christ and Apollo* (New York 1960), p. 5.

last word is still to be spoken. Parts of the world-story are told in the future tense. The Gospels end with attention eagerly directed to the future. The parables of Jesus are open-ended in the sense that the upshot is left as a challenge to the hearer.

The parable of the Good Samaritan does, of course, as an anecdote run to its conclusion. The traveller who was stripped and beaten is safe in the inn and his lodging has been paid for. But the story is not just told as a remarkable incident in the interest of curiosity or entertainment. The hearer is drawn into the middle of the little drama when it is as yet undecided. For Jesus inquires: 'Which of these three, do you think, proved neighbour to the man who fell among robbers?' And in conclusion, 'Go and do likewise.' Similarly with the parable of the Prodigal Son, the story is presumably ended so far as the younger brother is concerned. But what about the older brother? And how about ourselves?

In a similar way the hearer is led to identify himself with the wise or the foolish builder, with the wise or the foolish virgins. For us the outcome of the parables is still in the future. Similarly in the case of the early Christian confessions: they end as our later creeds do with expectation of the Last Act.

Thus the stories of the New Testament, whether the total story of Paradise Lost and Paradise Regained, or the most minute story like that of the widow who cast all that she had into the treasury—her whole living or life—these stories span our lives and wait our answer. To use a slang expression, they 'put us on the spot'. The stories are so graphic that we are bound hand and foot. Our consciences must stand and deliver. What is interesting here is the suggestion that it takes a good story to make people realize what the right thing to do is. The road to a moral judgment is by way of the imagination! One is tempted to say that aesthetics and ethics are not so far apart in the Gospel as is often supposed. They both have to do with the fitness of things.

III

We have indicated how large a part the narrative-mode has in the New Testament. We have drawn attention to different kinds of narratives in different parts of the New Testament. We have suggested how natural a speech-form this is for the Gospel, and how the New Testament stories involve the hearer and the reader to this day. We wish now to look at two story-types in particular: the anecdotes about Jesus in our Synoptic Gospels; and his own parables, discussed in the next chapter.

First, the anecdotes in the Synoptic Gospels. Apart from the sayings of Jesus these Gospels include many short narratives about him. They once circulated separately. One can recognize the way they have been strung together with loose transitions and summaries. When we look at them separately and one by one, we can penetrate back into the earlier stages of oral transmission. We have anecdotes about Jesus' healings and exorcisms, about his collisions with his adversaries, about his relations with his disciples or with outsiders including Samaritans and gentiles. We have anecdotes involving a debate-situation, anecdotes that come to a climax with some trenchant pronouncement. There are also episodes of the closing days of his life which are told, here, in closer sequence.

These kinds of stories evidently played an important part in the oral speech-patterns of the earliest Christians just as they form an important part of our written Gospels. Of course, the anecdote is a universal form. We find men telling stories wherever men talk at all. But these stories often have rather distinctive features. Many of the reports about Jesus were evidently condensed and polished in a particular way in the course of repeated telling. Nothing remains except the main point and what little else is needed to bring it out. In such stories the motive clearly is not just vivid evocation of an incident or storytelling for its own sake, but something more fateful. On the other hand, some of the narratives are more colourful and detailed and one can suspect the hand of a later Christian storyteller or haggadist, or, as we say, an embroiderer. Some of these stories have both the shape and spirit of visionary transactions and reflect Jewish models. Certainly some of these anecdotes go as far back as any speech elements in the life of the Church, indeed, to Jesus himself.

Let us take one characteristic healing narrative, the account in Mark 10.46–52 of Jesus' cure of the blind Bartimaeus at the gate of Jericho.[1]

[1] Martin Dibelius includes this among his 'Old Stories' ('Paradigms'), that is, among those narrative-units to which he assigns the greatest antiquity. (Cf. his *Message of Jesus Christ*, New York 1939, pp. 19, 138, 143, 166 f.) Bultmann is much more sceptical in his discussion of it (*Die Geschichte der Synoptischen Tradition*, 4 Auflage, Göttingen 1958, p. 228). He rightly notes suspicious secondary features in this *Heilungswunder*: the naming of the person cured; the skilful adaptation of the healing to a Jericho setting; the acclamation of Jesus as 'Son of David' in

And they came to Jericho; and as he was leaving Jericho with his disciples and a great multitude, Bartimaeus, a blind beggar, the son of Timaeus, was sitting by the roadside. And when he heard that it was Jesus of Nazareth, he began to cry out and say, 'Jesus, Son of David, have mercy on me!' And many rebuked him, telling him to be silent; but he cried out all the more, 'Son of David, have mercy on me!' And Jesus stopped and said, 'Call him.' And they called the blind man, saying to him, 'Take heart; rise, he is calling you.' And throwing off his mantle he sprang up and came to Jesus. And Jesus said to him, 'What do you want me to do for you?' And the blind man said to him, 'Master, let me receive my sight.' And Jesus said to him, 'Go your way; your faith has made you well.' And immediately he received his sight and followed him on the way.

What would this story convey as it was told and retold orally well before there were any written gospels? For its meaning we should put it in the context of the post-Resurrection faith. The believers lived in vivid realization of the time of fulfilment. The Old Testament promises of God's salvation were there and then coming to pass. These were the times when, as we read in Isa. 35.5–6:

> Then the eyes of the blind shall be opened,
>   and the ears of the deaf unstopped:
> then shall the lame man leap like a hart,
>   and the tongue of the dumb sing for joy.

But such salvation in the order of physical well-being was only one aspect of the general redemption. The cure of Bartimaeus was then a dramatic sign of what God was bringing to pass. Like other wonders in what we call the natural order and like certain parables of Jesus it conveyed the truth that God had bared his mighty arm and wrought salvation: being thus a small companion piece to the Resurrection-drama itself. This small anecdote was the Gospel in miniature. It dramatized the world-renewing favour and omni-

---

seeming conflict with the '*rabboni*' of v. 51. 'It is hardly possible to recognize an underlying original miracle-story narrated in the appropriate style.' We can, indeed, recognize such evidences of reshaping. Vivid details and dramatic visualization often argue rather for later imaginative editing than for eyewitness actuality. But the original fateful kerygmatic core that called for repetition in any Christian milieu could well have been the exceptional pressingness and urgency of the blind man's plea as expressive of his faith, a plea that refused to be silenced by the bystanders. The special feature in the story here is that 'many rebuked him, telling him to be silent' (v. 48). This detail (cf. the disciples' initial resistance to the bringing of the children to Jesus, Mark 10.14) does not have the colour of a retrospective theological or polemic motif. The charge against the Pharisees in Matt. 23.13 and Luke 11.52 is analogous, but *its* retelling in the oral tradition continued to have a polemic motive.

potence of God, the divine fiat of him who 'gives life to the dead and calls into existence the things that are not'.

This type of story is called a 'paradigm' or model, because it caught up in itself the import of the Good News. For the first believers it was a condensation of their faith. It would be an error to limit its significance to the physical healing. When the blind beggar, Bartimaeus, pressed his cry, 'Jesus, Son of David, have mercy on me!' he spoke for all who looked for the new age and its redemption. The special case of blindness here is secondary to the generic situation that human life is set about with what we call fatality and the inexorable. The reporting of the episode in the Early Church renewed the tensions of faith and their overcoming: on the one hand the sense of desperation of the human condition, and on the other the unlimited joy and surprise at the finger of God in the land of the living.

> He hath broken the gates of brass,
> And cut the bars of iron in sunder. (Ps. 107.16.)

The healing and others like it had this more general significance already in the activity of Jesus himself. His particular sayings and deeds took on their significance from the total context of his errand. The Early Church saw these in the light of his Resurrection, but this perspective did not basically affect their meaning.

To understand rightly the narratives of miraculous healings and deliverances in the Gospels we need, therefore, to bear in mind several considerations. In the first place we should recognize the Old Testament expectations and predictions with respect to God's compassionate acts in the New Age. These anticipations so far as they envisage actual healings were no doubt in part poetic and even hyperbolic: the raising of the dead to life, for example, could be metaphorical as in the case of Ezekiel's valley of dead bones. But these anticipations no doubt conditioned the scope of Jesus' dealings with the needy as well as coloured the later reports. We should also recall that for the thinking of that day there was no sharp distinction between physical and moral distress: illness, adversity, destitution, bondage and death were all of a piece, and salvation involved all of these at once. Finally we should recognize that intervention for the individual could not be seen as an isolated case—as in those instances recounted in contemporary pagan healings—but as a manifestation of a general redemption for the whole people of God.

We may well pause here to ask what the interpretation of such a

story means today. We have many such anecdotes in the Gospels of
how Jesus cured men's infirmities and with a word or a touch.
Modern readers are apt to read such accounts and to reflect upon
the 'love of the marvellous' of the early Christians or their 'pious
credulity'. Or students of the history of religions note the characteristic way in which extraordinary happenings and mysterious answers
to prayer get themselves told. What is more regrettable is the reaction
of the man or woman whose sense of helplessness may only be confirmed by a story like this one. The New Testament can even seem
to mock our impotence with its accounts of wholly exceptional rescues
and interventions. There is no question that the Gospels and Christianity itself occasion impatience if not bitterness because of such
narratives, or rather of the way in which they are understood.

What we have said should, however, have made it clear that we
have here a wrong approach to the accounts of Jesus' healings,
exorcisms and raisings of the dead. No doubt wonderful things were
done by him. But such reports are misread if taken out of the original
context we have described. The first Christians no doubt believed
that healing by faith and prayer sometimes took place. But their
main interest went deeper and their faith was more revolutionary.
Jesus announced the overthrow of Satan's whole reign and the
transformation of the world, as did his followers. Evidences of this
were seen in striking particular episodes, but above all in the new
life of the reborn and the Spirit. This meant that the more general
fatalities and impasses of our human nature were overcome in faith
and in anticipation.

Robert Penn Warren in his volume, *Promises*,[1] well sets up the
issue in a poem, 'The Child Next Door'. The Italian child in question
is defective, a cretin or monster. The beautiful twelve-year-old sister
who takes care of her has been able to train her to make the Italian
gesture of greeting with her hand. The poet is overcome with the
abyss between this enormity on the one hand and the playful device
on the other. He is revolted at this simulation that all is well and can
so easily be made well. Protesting, the poet exclaims with reference
to the beautiful sister:

> Fool, doesn't she know that the process
> Is not that joyous or simple, to bless or unbless
> The malfeasance of nature or the filth of fate?

[1] *Promises: Poems 1954–1956* (New York: Random House, 1955, 1957). 'The
Child Next Door' is on p. 5.

> Can it bind or loose, that beauty in that kind
> Beauty of benediction?

And the poet thinks of 'how empires grind, stars are hurled', and returns the greeting grimly, remarking to himself: 'This is the world.'

Now what is the implication of Jesus' cure of Bartimaeus for the case of this cretin in Warren's poem? Are we to think that if those concerned had faith enough the child could be made normal? Even if we rightly recognize the connection between faith and health of mind and body, Christians are often open to derision because they blandly refuse to look evil in the face, and find excuses even in Scripture for blinking what Warren here calls the 'malfeasance of nature and the filth of fate', and what he elsewhere speaks of as the 'turpitude of time'. Jesus' healings do, indeed, bear upon these aspects of life—all that seems cruel and immitigable—its fortuitous fatalities, whether the death of the young, incurable diseases, psychological disabilities and other victimizations. But we misunderstand his cures of the blind and the paralysed and the lepers if we see them only as individual cases of wonder-working, just as we deny their full significance if we take them only as expressions of compassion and satisfy ourselves with the statement that his love was the real miracle.

We should rather read these stories of his healings in the full gospel-context. The greater meaning to which they all point is that of the deliverance of all men, whether blind or not, lepers or not, whether sane or insane. The New Testament ministry of Jesus had to do not just with the driving out of demons from the few but with the dispossession of Satan generally. The several particular stories of how Jesus healed and raised the dead exhibit the ultimate omnipotence of grace. Each such narrative takes us to the place where human hungers and impulses meet a stone wall, where our petitions and intercessions seem to fall on deaf ears. Robert Penn Warren's poem states this situation.

But these Gospel stories also take us to that place in the total saving drama where we find a door opening in the wall and the bars of iron giving way. The fact is that when it is to the Christ that we cry 'Help!'—or with Bartimaeus: 'Jesus, Son of David, have mercy on me', and 'Master, let me receive my sight'—in this act we are engaged in what T. S. Eliot calls 'the purification of the motive in the ground of our beseeching'. And this is the condition of all salvation. The deepest self needs to be brought into play.

Thus whether or not we receive this or that petition for ourselves or for others, whether or not we find this or that particular cure or deliverance—what these miracle-stories point to is the *ultimate* confidence and guarantee, the transformation of the world pledged and foretasted in the last pages of each of our Gospels, and brought about precisely by him whose prayers were denied, namely that he should be spared the cup which he had to drink.

Thus all things are not well here about us, and there are many things that cannot here and now be made well. But the Christian can say with Eliot,

> And all shall be well and
> All manner of thing shall be well
> By the purification of the motive
> In the ground of our beseeching.[1]

IV

We have gone far afield with this example of the gospel anecdotes. Our first purpose was to show the significance of this rhetorical-form, the story, in the life of the Church in the oral period. Each one was a kind of gospel in miniature. Each episode was told and understood in the context of the total Good News. These stories were thus like pictures in a frame, and did not have their meaning then, nor do they have it today, without the frame.

But we can press back still farther to Jesus himself. Many of these incidents are historical. We can be sure here, too, that the meaning of his cures and exorcisms was then only rightly grasped in the frame of his total errand and message. Jesus was not just a healer or thaumaturge. His cures and exorcisms were aspects and dramatizations of the world-changing drama in which he was the principal.

Already, in the days of his ministry, we can be sure, stories about him and his disciples were circulating. We get overtones of this diffusion among his contemporaries of what entered into the later gospel tradition. What Jesus did and said in Galilee, we are told, came to the ears of John the Baptist in prison. Mark tells us that it came to the attention of 'the scribes who came down from Jerusalem' (3.22; cf. 3.7–8). Luke says of his first activities that 'there went out a fame of him through all the region round about' (4.14; cf. 1.65). We cannot press these statements, but we can be sure that the deeds of Jesus gave rise to talk about him, and that these reports,

---

[1] T. S. Eliot, 'Little Gidding', *Four Quartets* (New York 1943).

as to this day, confronted men with problems. Jesus' adversaries heard of his exorcisms and put them down to black magic just as others heard of John the Baptist's work and evaded its significance. John himself hearing of Jesus was in two minds about him.

Brief oral narratives about Jesus, then, go back to the beginning of the Gospel. It was not only his sayings that were passed on from mouth to mouth. His doings aroused interest. This fact is important in itself. The 'new' Gospel of Thomas gives us 114 sayings of Jesus, and only sayings. Its Gnostic author or authors evidently were chiefly interested in Jesus as a teacher of esoteric wisdom. The Jewish scribes of this period preserved by memory endless citations of what the famous rabbis said, and by comparison much less of what they did. It seems that there was some compelling reason for reporting on Jesus as a 'man of action' as well as a teacher.

What we really have here is the earliest beginning of our Gospels. This is important. We should not take it for granted that the Church must have produced gospels or must have accumulated stories about Jesus in action. We could well only have had traditions as to his sayings and as to his passion and Resurrection. From Paul's letters we would not suppose that the Church was specially interested in his doings or the course of his ministry.

It has been rightly suggested by scholars that the really important figures in the first decade or two of the Church were Christian prophets with their oracles and testimonies in the Spirit. The Twelve, no doubt, were important, but not in the way the Book of Acts and the New Testament have led us to picture them: as an authoritative college and as rehearsers of the deeds and sayings of Jesus. Their leadership, too, lay in their eschatological testimony and especially in their witness to the Resurrection. The Church was at first more caught up in apprehensions and revelations of the one glorified Jesus-Christ than in particular memories of Jesus as 'historical'. Its gaze was upon the future and not upon the past. It lived by the leadings of the Spirit and by the prophecies of the Old Testament now seen as in course of fulfilment. In this stage reports of Jesus' sayings and stories of his ministry were no doubt transmitted, but in the interests of present faith and future hope and not of biography. After the first prophetic and incandescent period came the stage of retrospect and instruction and debate and theology. Then the Christian teacher became more important and then the retrospective testimony of apostle and eyewitness came to the fore. We tend to get this all in reverse partly because our New Testament begins with the Gospels and because of the antedated picture that is given us in the Book of Acts.[1]

We recognize that it was only after a considerable period that the Church was led to the writing of gospels. Of course, the account of Jesus' death and Resurrection was essential from the beginning. But in the early decades the Christians did not share our modern point of view in a way that would have led them to a biographical interest in Jesus, a humanistic or a psychological or a descriptive interest. There surely was a personal interest, as we would say, but this attachment and cherishing was so fused with devotion to his mission and glory, and experienced in such different ancient sensibility, that it is hidden in our records.

In this early period, we are saying, much of the narrative which we now have in the Gospels was not of first concern. Much of it, moreover, was only beginning to be shaped. But we must make a distinction. There was one kind of report about Jesus that was essential from the beginning, one kind of story: those remembered incidents which made good what we can call the heart of the Gospel in the tangible actuality of his mission. Form-critics have rightly assigned priority, if not always actual historicity, to what they call the paradigm-form. These anecdotes are those in which the finger of God was there visible before men's eyes in grace and deliverance: typical episodes of redemption, anecdotes which carry the whole Gospel in a nutshell—victories over Satan, the demolishing of obstacles, including hard hearts, and the incursions of love. As we have seen in the case of the healing of Bartimaeus, these stories were miniature gospels, and were in that sense on the same level with the primordial witness to the Resurrection, and with the revelations that came to the Christian prophets. All these together made the first bridge from the Jesus of history to the Christ of faith. Many other kinds of stories about Jesus in the Gospels belong to very different and later strata.

We see, then, that one of the earliest and most important rhetorical forms in the Church was the story. This is theologically significant. The new movement of the Gospel was not to be identified with a new teaching or a new experience but with an action and therefore a history. The revelation was in an historical drama. The narrative

[1] See my 'Form-History and the Oldest Tradition', in *Neotestamentica et Patristica*, ed. by W. C. van Unnik and Bo Reicke (Leiden 1962), pp. 1–13.

mode inevitably imposed itself as the believers rehearsed the saving action, including particular scenes of it that played themselves out in the market-place or the Temple-court, at a dinner with guests or in a synagogue. The locus of the new faith was in concrete human relationships and encounters. Therefore the new community, living out a new kind of human and divine relationship, naturally rehearsed models of Jesus' actions and interactions, since it was through these that the saving work of God had initiated its course. With this kind of a God the story was the proper kind of witness even more than the saying or the dialogue. Exemplary stories about Jesus' ministry were repeated because they applied just as well to his followers after his departure as they still apply to hearers today.

Later, such brief anecdotes were gathered up into the longer story of the gospel-form, under new conditions. By this time and in this context the same stories were told with a special interest in the light they threw upon Christ himself or upon the problems of these followers of a later day. The same impulse that led to the writing of gospels—a focusing of faith upon the Jesus-story as such—this also led to subtle changes in the import of the particular anecdotes and even to changes in their form. In the early prophetic period of which we have spoken the recitals of Jesus' acts and words were told in a context of high eschatological expectation. In this mood the 'time' of Jesus was also the 'time' of his followers, and Jesus spoke and acted as still present. The post-Easter believer encountered the pre-Easter Jesus in the anecdotes reported. It is this crucial 'existential' and evangelical import of the 'old stories' relayed to us by the earliest Church which guarantees the authenticity of parts of our records. The so-called 'new quest' of the historical Jesus is based upon this approach. Here the real Jesus was contemporary in the oral period, though he was not, in their eyes, 'historical'. This primordial significance of the old anecdotes has never been lost; but with the passage of time the interest in the gospel tradition moved toward the biographical. New motives governed the transmission.

The earliest Christians, then, identified grace and revelation with the *present* Spirit and with the *present* Christ. Relevant traditions about Jesus' ministry coalesced with their post-Easter experience. But increasingly the Church read back the glory of the risen Christ into the days of his flesh and focused revelation upon his earthly career. This impulse made the writing of gospels inevitable. It also occasioned the reshaping of the original reports and the creation of new ones.[1] Thus we are not surprised to find that as the first formal strata of our later Gospels took shape, new story-elements and sayings of a less central kind—concerned with other than the primordial motifs—found their way into the collections. The prophetic activity in the Church could create as well as repeat. The increasing role of the Christian teacher reflects itself also in various areas now important to the community.

But all in all we can recognize the central place of the narrative-mode in the earliest Church and, indeed, throughout the whole New Testament period. The Christian movement stood or fell with the stories about Jesus, giving substance as they did to the larger history of God's dealings with men. As Jesus became little by little a figure of the past it was inevitable that gospels should be written, precisely to show the relation of his deed and deeds to the story of God with Israel and the world.

At this later stage the written Gospels anchored the Greek Gentile churches in concrete Palestinian origins. They linked both the joys and the trials of the Church Militant with earthly reality. Christian visions and hopes, then as now, are always in danger of becoming only poetry unless linked with on going discipleship. So it was in the first century. The elations of Pentecost and the Spirit took on irresponsible forms at Corinth and elsewhere. The Christ-story in the four Gospels safeguarded the new people against intoxication and pride. On the other hand, when the Church began to realize the costs of sustaining its way of life in the Empire, the Gospels evoked the needed model. The Christian could now relate his own history to the Christ-history, and find his own difficult role in the world-drama meaningful and glorious, since his role was caught up in that of the Son of Man himself. By means of the Gospels each of them could, and each one of us can, move back in time and walk with him along his way of victory through defeat; or could, as we can, bring him forward as a contemporary in the pilgrimage of a later day. In either case our own stories take on meaning, since they find their place in the larger story of which God is the author.

[1] James M. Robinson, *A New Quest of the Historical Jesus* (London 1959), pp. 53–55.

V

THE PARABLE

The art of the parable . . . is none other than that of bringing the hearer face to face with what it is to be human and thereby to make clear what it means for God to draw near.[1]

GERHARD EBELING

Brief and concise utterances fell from Him, for He was no sophist, but His Word was the power of God.

JUSTIN, *Apology* I, 14.5

AMONG THE NARRATIVE elements in the New Testament we now turn to the parables of Jesus. That storytelling had such a central place in the very beginning of the Gospel means more than may at first appear. It is not enough to say that Jesus used the form of the parable only as a good pedagogical strategy. It was not merely to hold the attention of his hearers that he told stories or took good illustrations out of his file. There was something in the nature of the case that evoked this rhetoric, something in the nature of the Gospel. At the very least there is the assumption that action is significant, and that the varied activities, pursuits, and vocations of men's life in nature are fateful.

Here we are reminded again that art-forms in any age are connected with basic assumptions about existence. The forms of literature in any society are governed, if not by theology, at least by world-attitudes of one kind or another. In the case of Jesus and his hearers the unconscious assumption is further that all life has the character of a story and of a plot. This world-story has many characters in it; this over-all plot has many sub-plots or episodes each of which reflects the significance of the whole. The new speech of Jesus carries this Jewish outlook to a new stage: the denouement of the world-story is come; the characters and their little histories are now in Act v; in fact, we hear twelve o'clock beginning to strike.

[1] *ZTK* 58 (1961), p. 135.

Antecedents of the parable or *mashal* before Jesus used it are found in the Old Testament, in the inter-testamental and apocalyptic writings, and especially in the sayings of the rabbis. The term meant first of all a comparison of some kind, but it included a wide variety of metaphors, similitudes, riddles, mysteries and illustrations. Many of these were brief tropes and we find such on Jesus' lips as when he speaks of the 'salt of the earth', or quotes, 'Physician, heal thyself'. But many of the Jewish parables have a narrative character as do many of those in the Gospels. Even here we find varieties. Some of the parables are straight narratives about a given individual case, ending with an application: the Good Samaritan, the Rich Fool; or sometimes about more than one person, as for example the Pharisee and the Publican. Here we have 'example-stories', not symbolic narrative. The point is in these cases that we should go and do likewise, or take warning by the given example. But in the parable of the Lost Sheep, on the other hand, the upshot is not that we should or should not go and do likewise. We have rather an extended image—the shepherd's retrieval of the lost sheep and his joy—a narrative image which reveals rather than exemplifies.

It is this revelatory character of Jesus' parables which is to be stressed.[1] Here Jesus is in line with the prophets and the apocalyptists as one who uses tropes or extended images to unveil mysteries, but above all to mediate reality and life. This is particulary clear in the so-called parables of the Kingdom like those of the sower and the mustard seed, in which Jesus mediates his own vision and his own faith. This understanding of Jesus' figures of speech is supported by our modern discussion of the metaphor in literary criticism. A simile sets one thing over against another: the less known is clarified by that which is better known. But in the metaphor we have an image with a certain shock to the imagination which directly conveys vision of what is signified.[2]

Yet we find also, of course, teaching-parables and polemic-parables, like those of the Prodigal Son or the Workers in the Vine-

---

[1] 'Thus the Christ preaching in parables appears as one who reveals mysteries, and not as one who instructs the multitudes'—Maxime Hermaniuk, *La parabole évangélique* (Louvain 1947), pp. 287–8. The same point is well stated by Günther Bornkamm, 'The parables are the preaching itself.'

[2] Even when Jesus' parables of the Kingdom are introduced by such a phrase as, 'The Kingdom of Heaven is like', we do not have true similes. It is generally recognized today that such introductory phrases only mean: the following story bears upon some aspect of the Kingdom. The parable of the sower, for example, is a developed image and a revealing metaphor, not an instructive simile or allegory.

yard in which the revelatory-image is employed to justify and defend Jesus' mission against misunderstanding or attack. The larger observation is that Jesus uses figures of speech in an immense number of ways. The variety of the parables is only one aspect of this variety. As Hermaniuk observes:

> By contrast with the rabbinic *meshalim*, the parables of Jesus are largely free of rigid and stereotyped formulas. They move with a great deal of freedom and are not constrained by any 'rule of the schools'.[1]

The use of narrative for purposes of comparison and analogy is found in full creative flexibility in Jesus' usage. Indeed, we may say that the term 'parable' is misleading, since it suggests a single pattern and often distorts our understanding of this or that special case.

For our purposes what is of special interest in the parables of Jesus is not only that he told stories but that these stories are so human and realistic. One can even speak of their secularity. The persons in question, the scenes, the actions are not usually 'religious'. It is true that Riesenfeld and others have urged that there is a large element of quasi-allegorical religious reference to Old Testament themes in the parables in such allusions as those to the king, the shepherd, the vineyard, the feast, the harvest, the act of sowing, etc.[2] On this view Jesus is not just evoking everyday human experience but is bringing in familiar images drawn from the ancient piety of Israel. This feature should not be exaggerated. We should not be so rigid as to exclude all such overtones. But the impact of the parables lay in their immediate realistic authenticity. In the parable of the Lost Sheep the shepherd is an actual shepherd and not a flash-back to God as the Shepherd of Israel or to the hoped-for Messiah who will shepherd Israel. To press these images in this way is to pull the stories out of shape and to weaken their thrust. In view, indeed, of the entire freedom with which Jesus uses pictures and comparisons we can

---

[1] *Ibid.*, p. 194. Full justice to the rabbinic parables requires that we recognize their occasional prophetic and non-casuistic character. It is not enough to say with Bornkamm: 'The rabbis also relate parables in abundance, to clarify a point in their teaching and explain the sense of a written passage, but always as an aid to the teaching and an instrument in the exegesis of an authoritatively prescribed text.' One can point to rabbinic parables which have as it were a kerygmatic character and stand apart from exegesis of the law; see especially the words ascribed to ben Zacchai on his death-bed, Berakoth 28b; Pirke Aboth 3.17; and Shabbath 153a, the banquet parable.

[2] Harald Riesenfeld, 'The Parables in the Synoptic and the Johannine Traditions', *Svensk Exegetisck Årsbok*, vol. 25 (1960), pp. 37–61. See also E. C. Hoskyns and N. Davey, *The Riddle of the New Testament* (New York 1931), pp. 177–91.

believe that he may in one case or another exploit such connotations. But this is exceptional. Where such allegorization of the parables appears, moreover, we can often recognize the hand of the later editors.

In the realism and the actuality of the parables we recognize Jesus the layman. It is not only human life that is observed but nature as well, or man in nature. This realism, moreover, has to do with things going on. This is a world in which as a matter of course things happen, men and women do things, one thing leads to another. And all this living is real and significant. The incidents may have some exceptional feature (for example, the three measures of meal in the parable of the leaven: 'enough to provide a meal for 162 persons', Dalman); or they may fix upon some critical life-situation (thus the unfaithful servant at the point of exposure); but they do have authentic verisimilitude.

It can be said, indeed, that this whole aspect of the parables, their naturalness and secularity, is only one side of them. There is also the application that Jesus gives to them, and that is moral and religious. But, nevertheless, we insist that these sharply-focused snapshots of life do reveal something very important about the storyteller himself and about the Gospel, apart from their further bearing.

Jesus, without saying so, by his very way of presenting man, shows that for him man's destiny is at stake in his ordinary creaturely existence, domestic, economic and social. This is the way God made him. The world is real. Time is real. Man is a toiler and an 'acter' and a chooser. The parables give us this kind of humanness and actuality. There is no romance or idealization here, no false mysticism, and no miracles, no impulse towards escape into fantasy or into sentimentality. We have stories, indeed, but they stay close to things as they are.

Now, of course, Jesus' thought moves on beyond the actual stories. They are only spring-boards or doors to something more important. There is the picture-side of the parable and there is the meaning or application. 'Go and do likewise.' Or, 'Pay the price.' Or, 'Trust in the harvest.' But there is no great leap out of the world here. The grace of the Gospel is just as 'down to earth' as is the father's treatment of the prodigal son. The second chance which is opened up for God's people is just as definite as that offered to the barren fig tree. And so in the other cases. We speak of Jesus' vivid parables and his skill in teaching. This is not to say enough. Jesus is not merely clarifying difficult ideas. He is leading men to make a judgment and to come to a decision. The stories are so told as to compel men to see things as they are, by analogy indeed. Sluggish or dormant awareness and conscience are thus aroused. The parables make men give attention, come alive and face things. And they do this by evoking men's everyday experience. It is implicit that a man can be saved where he is. And, indeed, the Gospel proposes not to substitute another world for this one, but to redeem and to transfigure the present world.

All this has been well said by Ernst Fuchs:

> Without question, it is from within this sphere of community and family living that Jesus speaks. It is from this life that he takes illustrations for his parables. We see men going about the streets and knocking at windows, we hear the sounds of their feasts; the peasant goes into the field, sows and reaps; the wife occupies herself with the small stretch of ground behind the house. We recognize the rich and the poor, the respected man and the scoundrel, gaiety and distress, sorrow and thanksgiving. But all that is not just scenery, not just 'material' for a poet . . . Jesus is not just using the details of this world as a springboard (*Anknuepfungspunkt*), but means precisely this 'world' . . . Jesus calls for faith and therefore decision. This decision places the man who responds on the side of God and the marvellous divine work in hand (Matt. 17.20). But: what the hearer now does, he does in the same area of daily life that Jesus evokes so vividly and plastically in his sayings and parables![1]

There is another way to come at the parables. Men in all kinds of societies and religions tell stories and tell them for their lessons. We shall agree, moreover, that there is nothing unique about the vividness and concreteness with which human life is struck off in Jesus' parables. We can find this in Homer, in the decorations of ancient Egyptian tombs and elsewhere. But there is a great deal of difference as to depth or superficiality with which man is presented. Some good stories—and we can think here also of the novel or the epic—turn upon the fortunes of men, the ups and downs of life, success and failure, surprise and disappointment. The appeal of such stories and of such wisdom as they have is identified especially with the plot and its surprises. Other good stories turn on the perennially interesting topic of character in men, their varying traits and types, and the consequences of these. Or a good story may have its chief appeal in

[1] Ernst Fuchs, 'Das Neue Testament und das hermeneutische Problem', *ZTK* 58 (1961), p. 211.

the sheer surface delineation, the absorbing detail and concreteness of the portrayal.

In none of such fictions, however, do we necessarily have man and the enigma of man adequately presented. What especially may be missing is some sense of that secret of his being where he is a mixture of freedom and helplessness, of loneliness and entanglement, and where all this carries with it a consciousness of responsibility, and where man is sensitive not only to external approval or disapproval but to internal peace or shame.

The difference between various levels of fiction and the special Christian contribution is recognized in an authoritative way by André Gide in a passage in *Les Faux-Monnayeurs*:[1]

> It seems to me that one kind of tragic dimension has for the most part been missing in literature up until now. The novel has concerned itself with the strokes of fate, with good and bad fortune, with social interchanges, with the conflict of passions, with characters, but not at all with the essence of the human being.
> To carry the drama over to the moral plane—this, however, was the task of Christianity. Yet properly speaking, there is no such thing as a Christian novel. There are those which aim at edification, but that is not at all what I have in mind. It is a question of moral tragedy—of that kind which makes so momentous the text: 'If salt has lost its taste, how can its saltness be restored?' It is this kind of tragedy which concerns me.[2]

It is also to the point here to quote the great classicist Wilamowitz speaking of men as they appear in Homer. He observes that

> They charm us like children of Goethe's *Prometheus*: a race born to suffer and weep, to enjoy and be glad—and not to take account of good and bad, or of guilt and destiny as the case is similarly with their blessed kindred, the gods.[3]

Of course, in the Greek tragedies we get another kind of story and the mystery of man is profoundly stated by Aeschylus and Sophocles, as well as a sense of overruling justice. Without going into comparisons we can say that in the parables of Jesus men come before us in their moral mystery and in a perspective of divine severity and love. But what is *sui generis* is the way in which these deeper dimensions are married to such ordinariness and secularity. The deepest

---

[1] Paris: Gallimard 1925.
[2] P. 160.
[3] Introduction to the *Agamemnon* of Aeschylus, cited by G. Bornkamm, *Das Ende des Gesetzes* (Munich, 1952), p. 173.

mysteries of providence and destiny are at home with this naturalness. Here we have in Jesus' sayings the counterpart of his own person
and presence among men: not as a philosopher, priest or scribe but
as an artisan, not in the desert or in the temple but in the market-
place.

All this bears, too, on the style of the parables. Precise observation, actuality of presentation, art beyond art in the telling. One can
compare Jesus' parables in the matter of form with those of the
rabbis. One can note the particular twists given them by the evangelists or in such later versions as we find in the Gospel of Thomas
or in the Church Fathers. The rabbinic parables are often beyond
praise for their purpose. But as Joachim Jeremias writes, those in
our Synoptic Gospels 'reveal a definite personal character, a unique
clarity and simplicity, a matchless mastery of construction'.[1]

This formal uniqueness is related to the urgency of Jesus' errand.
The rabbis can use the parable in illustration of a wide variety of
topics and often therefore with less sense of import and more ex-
pansiveness or colourfulness (also in interpretive supplement) and
more tendency toward allegory. The parables of Jesus, in addition
to their revelatory character, are shaped more consistently towards a
direct personal appeal or challenge, and their sobriety of style and
sharpness of focus serve well the fatefulness of the issue in view. We
can recognize this even if we disregard such introductions as,
'Listen!' or such conclusions as, 'He that hath ears to hear, let him
hear!' We cannot but be surprised by the fact that such incomparable human and naturalistic and artistic portrayal of human life
should come to us from one who spoke out of an acute eschatological
crisis. Jesus saw men on the brink of world-judgment and transformation. Yet we have in the parables no stridency and no fanaticism.
Must one not say that it was the very intensity of his world-dissolving
vocation which accounts for the consummate shape of these sayings,
these crystals of human language? His revolutionary role and message
had its high-pitched aspects and accents, but these never took the
form of shrillness, of the esoteric or the angelic. The one feature of
his parables which echoes his eschatological challenge is the trait of
hyperbole which often appears here as in his teaching generally.
This is the only point at which they appear to diverge from realism,
and yet only in such a way as to suggest the element of surprise or
contrast in the situation.

[1] *The Parables of Jesus* (London 1954), p. 10.

II

To know who Jesus was it is not enough to ask what he said about himself or his mission. In his modes of speech we may recognize yet another clue to the mystery of his being. In certain ages of culture we know how earlier artistic forms, whether in painting or music or poetry, come to a moment of perfection in some great master. He is able both to exploit all the initiatives of his predecessors and at the same time to relate himself and the forms he employs to a new occasion. So in Jesus, it is as though many ancient tributaries of speech, many styles, merged in him. The discourse of prophet, lawgiver and wise man meet in him. He unites in himself many roles.

The most obvious reconciliation of opposites or of differences here is that of the wise man and the seer. We find at home in his speech the parable of the wisdom tradition as well as the prophetic oracle. Jesus' indebtedness to the wisdom tradition of his people is evident not only in the parable form which he uses but also in his aphorisms, which he uses in a variety of sophisticated forms.

On the other hand, his indebtedness to the prophetic tradition appears in a variety of ways. The prophet is the spokesman of the potent and dynamic word, the word that acts. For a right understanding of this kind of utterance we can go to simpler cultures where men recognize the mystery of language. In the Old Testament we see the quasi-magical power of the blessing and the curse, the promise and the woe, the ban and the name-giving. In Jesus' speech this depth of the word reappears. His beatitudes are not sentimental congratulations but, like the woes that accompany them, oracular exclamations. The seven beatitudes in the Book of Revelation illuminate their character and context. Jesus' prophetic-eschatological pronouncements are loaded with dynamite and represent the ethicizing and the spiritualizing of the ancient tradition of the spell, the charm, and the magic command.

Yet Jesus himself is neither sage nor apocalyptist, though he uses both traditions. In a sovereign way he transforms and reconciles these different rhetorics and, we can add, the tradition of lawgiver. We recall the saying of Jeremiah: 'The law shall not perish from the priest, nor counsel from the wise, nor the word from the prophet' (Jer. 18.18). We find these all—all these styles—in Christ. We are reminded of the lines from Shakespeare's sonnet:

> What is thy substance, whereof art thou made,
> That thousands of strange shadows on thee tend!

We can pursue this further. Nearest of kin to the parables of Jesus are those of the Jewish rabbis. But the parable or *mashal* as they used it was rooted in the wisdom tradition of Israel,[1] associated with Solomon, but going far back beyond him in the ancient love of clever speech and trope among the Hebrews and especially the Egyptians. It is a moving thought that the incomparable and destiny-fraught parables of Jesus are directly linked with generations and millennia of human delight in the apt word and the felicitous image.

Now if the parables of Jesus came out of the wisdom tradition of Israel, we also know today that apocalyptic was closely related to wisdom. If Solomon was seen as the founder of proverbial wisdom, Enoch, for example, was a chief representative of wisdom of another kind.[2] Jesus' eschatological outlook and imagery were related to the latter as his parables were to the former. He united both styles and brought both into direct relation with the realities of his time.

Indeed, there are parables in the apocalyptic literature of Judaism and in its inter-testamental writings which illuminate Jesus' use of this form. In the Book of Enoch the term *mashal* is prominent in the sense of a 'revelation of the secrets of God concerning the economy of salvation, relative to the person and work of the Messiah as well as to the destiny of the good and the evil'.[3] Thus in Enoch (as in the oracles of Balaam in chs. 23–24 of Numbers) a parable or *mashal* means a prophetic unveiling of the secrets of the future. In inter-testamental Judaism there was a tendency for the older categories to be merged—law and wisdom, but also wisdom and prophecy or apocalyptic vision.[4] It is true that Jesus' parables of the kingdom are not strictly unveilings of the secrets of the heavenly realm in the sense of its geography or its angelic and demonic orders. But they

---

[1] The *mashal* is a dominant feature of the biblical wisdom literature. In this literature, it is true, we have mainly single tropes, expanded proverbs, and meta-phorical aphorisms rather than developed stories. But the Old Testament and ancient tradition of the East provide ample evidence of the story-parable.

[2] See Pierre Grelot, 'La legende d'Henoch dans les Apocryphes et dans la Bible', *Recherches de Science Religieuse* 46, pp. 5–26; 181—210.

[3] Hermaniuk, *op. cit.*, p. 130.

[4] See Raymond E. Brown, 'The Pre-Christian Semitic Concept of "Mystery",' *Catholic Biblical Quarterly* 20/4 (Oct. 1958), pp. 417–43; and 'The Semitic Background of the New Testament *mystērion*, I and II', *Biblica* 39 (1948), pp. 426–48; 40 (1959), pp. 70–87.

have the character of prophetic revelation,[1] as is not the case with the
rabbinic parables or most of them. On the other hand, they are like
the latter in that they are firmly planted in human life. The parables
of Jesus thus draw upon both the wisdom mode of the rabbis and
that of the seers. But in this connection also we must say that a
greater than Jonah is here and a greater than Solomon.

The rhetorical perfection of the parables of Jesus could lead a
reader to think of him as essentially a teacher and as a rather dis-
passionate one at that, as an artist. We do not easily reconcile such
fastidious concern with form with eschatological fervour and passion.
Prophetic inspiration, we think, must necessarily give us outbursts of
passion rather than the kind of classic rhetoric of these parables.
Some are tempted, therefore, to say that the Jesus of the parables
alone is the real Jesus, and that the fanciful and perfervid sayings of
an apocalyptic kind cannot be authentic. The Jesus of the parables
is sane; the Jesus who speaks of the Son of Man coming with the
clouds is fanatical. The Jesus of the parables is a true humanist; the
eschatological Jesus is a cloudy visionary.

In such judgments we are misled by modern categories of classic
and romantic. We associate artistic forms of speech like those of the
parables with cool and polished workmanship, repeatedly worked
over and brought to perfection. We associate what seem eloquent
outbursts of vision with unpremeditated inspiration and even
ecstasy. Our own predisposition may lead us to prefer one to the
other. With respect to Jesus, in any case, we are puzzled. We have
on the one hand the parables and such patterned and strophic
sayings as those evoking the lilies of the field and the fowl of the air.
And we have, on the other hand, such sayings as: 'I beheld Satan as
lightning fallen from heaven. Behold, I give unto you power to tread
on serpents and scorpions, and over all the powers of the enemy:
and nothing shall by any means hurt you' (Luke 10.18–19); or
'Then shall they see the Son of man coming in the clouds with great
power and glory. And then shall he send his angels, and shall gather
together his elect from the four winds, from the uttermost part of the
earth to the uttermost part of heaven' (Mark 13.26–27).

But what we should recognize, as Ernst Käsemann has said, is that

---

[1] At this point and elsewhere in this chapter I am indebted to the discussions
in the graduate New Testament Seminar at the Harvard Divinity School, which
dealt with the topic of the Gospel parables in the fall semester of 1961–62 under the
chairmanship of Professor Krister Stendahl.

felicity and sophistication of form is perfectly compatible with prophetic and, indeed, extempore utterance.[1] Thus the parable of the sower, for instance, can well be seen as prophetic rather than sapiential. The aesthetic balance of Jesus' sayings about serving two masters or about the strait gate and the broad way, similarly, can represent prophetic improvisation. In any case they have the immediate impulse that goes with their oral character. The point is ✓ that Jesus transcends all these dichotomies. The same issue arises with respect to the hymns and oracles produced by the Church after the Resurrection, powerful and concentrated rhetorical utterances which we find cited both in the Epistles and in the Gospels. These have poetic form. For example, we can cite the jubilant formulas found in chapters two and three of the Apocalypse of which one instance is:

> To him that overcometh will I grant to
> sit with me in my throne,
> even as I also overcame, and am set
> down with my Father in his throne (3.21).

Or we can cite as such an oracle the words found on the lips of Jesus:

> Whoever says a word against the Son of Man will be forgiven;
> but whoever speaks against the Holy Spirit will not be forgiven,
> either in this age or in the age to come (Matt. 12.32).

Now Käsemann rightly says with regard to such early Christian apocalyptic testimonies:

> Primitive Christianity as its hymns and its 'he that overcometh' sayings
> in Revelation show, assigned precisely to the Spirit the power to combine kerygmatic concentration and artistic form.[2]

Returning to the parables of Jesus, we conclude that their artistic form does not make them in any way incompatible with Jesus' eschatological sayings. Nor should we think of them as artistically premeditated in contrast with other sayings seen as ejaculations or outbursts. Even in the case of the parables we are confronted with

---

[1] 'Die Anfänge christlicher Theologie', *ZTK* 57 (1960), p. 174, and see there his footnote 2.

[2] *Ibid.* Further, with reference to the sayings of Jesus about Jonah and the Queen of the South, Matt. 12.41 ff. Käsemann writes, 'Only a false conception of inspiration as leading to an uncontrolled outburst of feeling can argue from [such poetic form] against this as an instance of prophecy.'

that immediacy and presence of the speaker which we have stressed in connection with the oral features of all Jesus' communication.

III

Let us select for attention those parables which are usually spoken of as the parables of the Kingdom. We find these in the fourth chapter of Mark, the parables of the sower, the seed growing of it-self, the mustard seed. And we select from the thirteenth chapter of Matthew also those of the leaven, the hidden treasure and the pearl of great price. We extricate these parables from the contexts in which the evangelists place them, and we try to identify their original form by taking account of any parallels and of recastings. We also disregard for the time being the interpretations assigned to Jesus of the parable of the sower.

Now we have good reason to believe that we have reached bed-rock with this material. There is wide agreement that it is in the parables that we can feel confidence that we hear Jesus of Nazareth speaking. We have a natural desire to identify precisely his authentic words, the *ipsissima verba*. The importance of this should not be over-estimated. We can know Jesus historically through the eyes and through the hearts of his immediate followers even if they do not remember his words exactly and even when they quite understand-ably adapt, supplement and generalize them, not to speak of those which they forget or pass over. Even when they put words in his mouth these, too, may convey to us the reality of the founder in what is most essential. Jesus' creative speech was so fresh and significant that it could, as it were, breed speech true to itself. We have an analogy of this phenomenon when we say that certain stories about Abraham Lincoln may not be authentic, but they are true to Lincoln.

Yet we naturally seek to identify the actual words of Jesus. One of the criteria for this is form, and here evidently the parable offers a very tangible example. The characteristic design, the tight form, of these utterances helped to guarantee them against change and supplementation. A coherent image-story is resistant to change. One can press putty into different shapes but not a crystal. A crystal can pick up foreign material but we can recognize the difference. Here especially if a thing is well said there is only one way to say it, as in a poem. These parables of Jesus have an organic unity and coherence. They come down through retelling protected by their shape and hardness like quartz nuggets in a stream. This organic unity, say of the parable of the seed growing of itself, or of the sower, derives from the fact that each one represents an imaginative vision. All the aspects fall into place. Each one is a little drama seen as a whole.

One can raise the question whether followers of Jesus could not have created one or other of these parables. We do not need to be jealous for Jesus in this respect. We should be ready to admit that a sonnet ascribed to Shakespeare or a painting ascribed to Rembrandt is not as we say genuine. But there are criteria. Such criteria have always something of the subjective about them. As a matter of fact, there is some reason to think that the parable of the tares is not genuine. Such tests are verisimilitude, force, relevance, dependence on other parables, and in the case of the parable of the tares all these considerations converge to arouse our suspicions. The acid tests for Jesus' parables are what I would call focus and depth. There is no blurring in them or incongruity. Moreover, they are not discursive. All this springs from the depth of concern and intensity of vision. It is not fair, perhaps, to contrast Paul here, since he is discoursing in another vein. But it is well known that his metaphors drawn from building operations or agriculture reflect a different kind of inspiration. There are elements of incongruity in them arising from an allegorical procedure, just as there are in some of Jesus' parables in those aspects which reflect later supplementation by his followers.

Let us return to this matter of the criteria for the authenticity of Jesus' sayings. We find our confidence at the maximum in his parables. I would go further and say: in certain kinds of his parables, especially these parables of the Kingdom. Some of his parables, such as these, are in their nature more closely knit, more clearly shaped by a single vision. They are therefore less subject to modification. They can be interpreted like the parable of the sower, but they cannot easily be revised; and if they are revised the revision betrays itself. But Jesus' illustrative stories have great variety. He used images with sovereign freedom and in very different veins. Therefore there are some of what we call his parables which are indeed distinctive and powerful but looser in texture, not requiring the same inevitability and design. And there are some whose flexible variation in the telling is already clearly evident in the Gospels as well as in the later Church: such parables as those of the Watchful Servants, the Feast, the Pounds or Talents. Such parables may often have been occasioned by particular pedagogical or controversial occasions.

Their mintage was therefore different. They lent themselves to new applications. It is more difficult to recover the original wording.

Another formal consideration bearing on the authenticity of Jesus' parables takes us farther afield. It is the role of image and metaphor in his speech generally. In the parables we have action-images. But these are only one kind of metaphor, extended metaphor. Jesus' communication, just because it is fresh and dynamic, is necessarily plastic. Now we know that a true metaphor or symbol is more than a sign, it is a bearer of the reality to which it refers. The hearer not only learns about that reality, he participates in it. He is invaded by it. Here lies the power and fatefulness of art. Jesus' speech had the character not of instruction and ideas but of compelling imagination, of spell, of mythical shock and transformation. Not just in an aesthetic sense but in the service of the Gospel. Now, just as Jesus used trope and metaphor in the most varied way, so with his narrative-images. But in either case we have a criterion for his authentic words in the force and significance of the imagery.

With this question of the significance of the imagery we can return to the parables of the Kingdom. Let us have in mind first Mark's parables of the sower, of the seed growing of itself, and of the mustard seed. We have seen that with respect to form and texture they fall into the type of action-images; their minting represents a single act of total vision; they are prophetic in character rather than discursive or argumentative.

Now, is it enough to say that in the parable of the sower, for example, Jesus offers encouragement to his disciples over against the inevitable setbacks and disappointments of the preaching of the Kingdom; the farmer loses some seed here, some seed there, but in the outcome there is abundant—even super-abundant—harvest? If we read the parable somewhat prosaically this is where we come out. And this kind of reading soon passes over into various applications and point for point allegory, all of which may be instructive but lacking in any momentous significance. This would have meant then that Jesus led his disciples and ourselves to trust in God's overruling of difficulties. But this parable is surely not just an example of what happens every day offered as an encouragement. This would be banal. The hearer could say: 'Well, sometimes the farmers are re-warded this way, sometimes not.' Thus this kind of interpretation, I repeat, really offers only a kind of commonplace. Taken in this way the parable itself falls down. As Ernst Fuchs has observed, the farmer hopes that he will have a large crop; he usually does; but there is nothing in the nature of the case that guarantees it; drought or other calamity may ruin the year's operation. Therefore the illustration in itself offers no cogent assurance to the faith of the disciple. At the best in these terms the parable says what we can hear on all sides from men of courage and hopefulness.

Similarly with the parable of the seed growing of itself, and we confine ourselves to the verses Mark 4.26–28:

> And he said, 'The Kingdom of God is as if a man should scatter seed upon the ground, and should sleep and rise night and day, and the seed should sprout and grow, he knows not how. The earth produces of itself, first the blade, then the ear, then the full grain in the ear.'

Again we take this too often in a banal sense. Jesus' disciples learned that they could trust the secret working of God. In the parable of the mustard seed, we have the same confidence inspired, though here the emphasis falls on the disproportion between the small beginnings and the great outcomes. But this again can be banal; we have heard it before.

Fortunately we usually see more in these parables than this because we come at them in the context of the Christian faith, the Christian mystery. But we must go all the way in this matter of context and see them in Jesus' own situation. Then their real authority and power emerge. It is Jesus' own certain faith that paints in the feature of the great harvest. The formal felicity and coherence of these parables reflect the intensity of his own vision. The parable of the sower is a prophetic and not a discursive parable, a metaphor of faith. The realism, however, testifies to the fact that that faith and expectation are identified with daily life and with God's operation there. The disciples are heartened not by a homiletic illustration drawn from nature but by Jesus' impartation to them of his own vision by the power of metaphor. For us, too, to find the meaning of the parable we must identify ourselves with that inner secret of Jesus' faith and faithfulness. To quote again from Fuchs:

> The distinctive feature in the teaching aspects of Jesus' proclamation is the analogical power with which tacitly he sets forth himself, his own obedience, as a measure for the attention of his disciples.[1]

[1] *Hermeneutik* (Bad Cannstatt 1958), p. 228. This statement and its elaboration by Fuchs locate one focus of the contemporary discussion of the parables, especially in connection with the new quest of the historical Jesus. Cf. Fuchs, *Hermeneutik*, section 17, and 'Bemerkungen zur Gleichnisauslegung', in *Zur Frage nach dem historischen Jesus* (Tubingen 1960), pp. 136–42.

Objection may be raised to this understanding of the parables which links their significance with Jesus himself. There has been too much of a dogmatic view according to which the figure and authority of Christ is read into and forced upon the parables. Thus the sower in these parables is identified with Christ. But he is also in other parables identified as the pearl of great price or even as the thief who breaks in when not expected, etc. We, for our part, are not insisting on a Christological interpretation of the parables in any such sense. But we are saying that they should be understood in relation to the speaker and the occasion; not in connection with his titles but in relation to his way and his goal.

If we bring in the twin parables of the treasure in the field and the pearl of great price we can enlarge our discussion. Let us quote the former:

> The kingdom of heaven is like treasure hidden in a field, which a man found and covered up; then in his joy he goes and sells all that he has and buys the field (Matt. 13.44).

As Joachim Jeremias says, the emphasis here is not on the value of the treasure nor on the sacrifice involved, but on the joy in the discovery. This joy feature is implicit in the seed parables with their sense of marvel and expectation, just as it comes to expression in the Beatitudes which are to be understood as congratulatory rather than hortatory.

The historical Jesus comes into better focus if we see him as using two media to proclaim the kingdom—in addition to his action, of course. On the one hand he used eschatological imagery and categories. 'The Kingdom of God is at hand.' He spoke of the judgment, the Messianic banquet, the life of the age to come, perhaps of the heavenly Son of Man coming with the clouds of heaven. All this was the available theological symbol of his time and place. But he said the same things in what we can call layman's language in his parables of the Kingdom, parables of judgment, etc. What does this mean except that he brought theology down into daily life and into the immediate everyday situation? Here is a clue for the modern preacher, indeed for the Christian whatever his form of witness.

In both his eschatological and his parable announcement we have the note of joy. Behind both again is the sense of the power and grace of God at work and the wonder and promise of the outcome. Jesus testifies to all this confidence in his parables but also to the requisite decision and devotion and, indeed, to the endurance and suffering involved. The parables we have been concerned with all involve an action, a narrative—associated with life as it is—and the features of waiting, endurance and striving are variously included. The full significance of all this is only lifted above the banal and commonplace if we recognize the momentousness of that to which Jesus himself witnesses. His eschatological language is one indication of it. The parables, even including their form, are another. The Church later identified this momentousness of the parables by finding in them the 'mystery' of the Kingdom of God.

I myself choose a trope or parable to suggest this significance of the Gospel and of the rhetoric of faith employed by Jesus. The French poet St-John Perse, in his address on the occasion of receiving the Nobel Prize for literature spoke of the power of language, especially of the power of the image-maker the poet. He had the audacity to compare that power with that of nuclear energy. He did not hesitate to set the fragile clay lamp of the poet over against the atomic oven as source of world-transformation. Unimagined futures lie folded as in a seed in a new creative word, in the birth of language, in an emerging myth.

This is a dim analogy of the power of the Gospel and of the dawning Kingdom of God as Jesus knew it and brought it to expression in his parables as well as in his eschatological sayings. It is this kind of authority, certainly, that voices itself in the seed-parables, aware of cost and ordeal but also of joy. If the poet's clay lamp is ultimately more determinative than the atomic oven, we hear in the Gospel also of a lamp set on a stand where it gives light to all in the house; and of a city which 'has no need of sun or moon to shine upon it, for the glory of God is its light, and its lamp is the Lamb' (Rev. 21.23).

The parables, finally, permit us to make one observation about the founder of Christianity which transcends our discussion hitherto. In these sayings we have the one element in the Gospels of any extent which after due sifting we can hold as original with little question. What do these sayings tell us about Jesus? They tell us that we have here a Jewish mind and heart at that precise point of the heritage where the particular religious tradition becomes indistinguishable from a universal humanity, where religion becomes secular without loss, where Israel becomes Adam, the law becomes the way of mankind, and the son of Abraham becomes the Son of man. The humanity and secularity of Jesus, it should be emphasized, is not, however, to be confused with humanist, romantic or aesthetic ideals, though it includes all that these quests seek. In the Jesus of the parables we have a humanity in which uniquely the heart of man is recognized, as is not the case in all such humanisms, and yet in a way which is universal.

VI

THE POEM

And they sing the song of Moses, the servant of God, and
the song of the Lamb, saying,
Great and wonderful are thy deeds,
O Lord God the Almighty!
Just and true are thy ways,
O King of the ages!

REV. 15.3

I will sing with my spirit and I will sing with the mind
also.

I COR. 14.15

WE HAVE SEEN how natural it was that genres like dialogue
and story should have an essential place in early Christian
rhetoric. In both forms the historical drama of God's dealing with men could come to expression. How is it with poetry?

Rhythmic speech, of course, plays a large part in all religions from
their earliest beginnings. It is a question then for us as to the kind
of poetry in the New Testament. That we have poetry at all, however, and playing an important role, is to be expected in view of what
we have said about the freedom and creativeness of the Gospel as
itself Word. From the beginning Christianity selected forms of utterance and communication that were dynamic.

Now it is true that the poem as an art-form has aesthetic conventions dictated by a tradition. A good poem in any cultural epoch is
a combination of convention and novelty, of received structure and
improvisation. The new speech-freedom of Jesus and his followers,
this new fruit of the lips and new range of meaning, inevitably
adopted the rhythmic mode. It is one of the primal categories of
human gesture. Basically oral, it has a somatic-dynamic character
like music and the dance. Yet only some kinds of poetry were
specially destined for Christian use: those that convey its personal
depth. Other veins of verse may even falsify the Christian consciousness.

Those modes of poetry that are at home in the new covenant include the historical: for example, the historical Psalms of Israel taken over into the Church, or Christian confessional hymns declaiming the career of the Redeemer. Later examples of this mode are found in the Christian use of epic as in *Paradise Lost*, or in rehearsals of this or that aspect of the story of salvation like Browning's 'A Death in the Desert' or Eliot's 'Journey of the Magi'. Another poetic mode that is congenial to the Gospel is the dramatic: for example, the answering voices of the Apocalypse, or, taken over from the old covenant, the forensic dialogue of the prophets, and the wrestlings with God in the Psalter. Modern examples would include such dramatizations of the Nativity scenes as we find in Auden's *Christmas Oratorio*, and Christian plays like Christopher Fry's *Sleep of Prisoners*. Other strains of poetry, lyric, elegiac, etc., are consonant with the faith only when they communicate its full personal reality. Private lyrical and mystical verse are therefore open to question. Many of our hymns betray a lack of Christian discrimination at this point.

We have here a parallel with the Christian use of the story. Jesus was not the first to use the parable. But, as we have seen, this genre took on a special character as he used it. The Gospel's story-forms, however artistic, have a formidable personal focus which distinguish them. Its poem-forms, similarly, focus upon the heart and its ultimate response to God. But this response takes place in the midst of the great world-change announced in the Gospel, and plastic and rhythmic language must be called forth to convey this level of experience. For it is poetry alone in all periods that can mediate that overcoming of law, fate and necessity which faith celebrates.

When we read Aesop's fables or Grimm's fairy tales we 'identify' ourselves with the action in such a way as to be entertained or caused to shudder. But when we read the parable of the Unmerciful Servant we face, if not the accusation, 'Thou art the man', at least the query, 'Art thou that man?' When we read the Hymn of Cleanthes or the Psalm of Akhnaton to the solar disc we may be lifted into self-forgetful contemplation and sympathy with all created things. But when we hear the doxologies of the Book of Revelation or the lyrics of the New Jerusalem, some more ultimate cry or hunger in us overhears pledges of that last word which will finally overrule all fates and tyrannies. The biblical poetry is ordered about the story of the Lord's deliverances, and these are always at least in the background of the recitations and songs of the New Testament as they are of our best hymns, spirituals, cantatas and and oratorios to this day.[1]

Thus the poem in Christianity has its special character. The spontaneity of its song is something other than the sheer impulse of man the maker in however refined a form. The Christian heart does indeed pass not only from prose to poetry, but from dialogue with God into the monologue of song. There is a place in Christian joy beyond good and evil. But the imagination and arts of the new people are always finally linked with and lifted by that knowledge of reality afforded by the Good News and its cost. 'The New Testament poem always moves towards accord with the divine Voice' (Fuchs). Even the song of the angels at the birth of Christ celebrates the plan of redemption and peace on earth for those whom God has chosen. The songs of the new race avoid on the one hand bloodless spirituality. They also avoid the carnal celebration of Adam's flesh. But the primal passions, appetencies and endowments of the creature are not denied; rather are they baptized and ordered. The corollaries of all this for poetic styles and images are many, and are to be identified wherever a Christian culture borrows pagan or secular expression.

To use the term 'poem' for the various New Testament passages with which we are here concerned is perhaps to beg the question. Our usual literary classifications are based on classical and Western practice. The arts of the Orient are not easily fitted into them. Different ages and cultures of men have produced different kinds of rhetorics. We should recognize that our Western categories are provincial. We have to make room for the No-plays of Japan in our view of drama, for the cave-paintings of the Dordogne and the sculpture of pre-Columbian America in our view of the graphic arts. In fact, we have been living now for half a century at least in the midst of constant fertilization of our aesthetics from non-Western arts. This

[1] 'The term "spiritual songs" itself indicates the fundamental difference between Christian and pagan hymns. The consciousness of a new element in the worship of God is perfectly clear in the designation, "a new song", which the Revelation employs (5.9; 14.3). This is supplied by the facts bound up with the Christ, the events of salvation-history. The song of the Christian Church is "new" in an absolute sense: Christians know that they stand in the midst of the occurrence of the fulfilment. The content of the primitive Christian hymns which have been handed down to us is not, therefore, subjective effusions of the emotions but they express in clear-cut sentences praise for the saving activity of God in Christ; hence they often have the character of a confession of faith'—G. Delling, *Worship in the New Testament* (London and Philadelphia 1962), pp. 87–88.

is also true of poetry. Ezra Pound and others have introduced us to
the poetry of ancient China. The anthropologists have enriched our
ideas of religious myth and saga. We should be more ready to make
a place in our 'poetic' for the verse forms of the ancient Near East
and of Scripture.

When we thus admit the wide variety of poetic styles our difficulties in defining poetry will be all the greater, and our difficulties
in distinguishing it from prose. The one test that we can rely on will
be that of rhythm and the associated state of excitement or enhance-
ment of consciousness, which often comes to expression as vision or
seeing. As Goethe said, poetry is *Schauen*.

II

The poetry of the New Testament is based on two different traditions, that of Hellenistic paganism and that of Israel.[1] Hellenistic
poetry had a variety of forms. But those which most influenced the
New Testament writers were on the one hand a kind of recitational
poetic prose, and on the other an antithetical oracular style. Both of
these patterns have influenced the literature of Hellenistic Judaism
as well as early Christian literature. On the other hand, the leading
features of traditional Hebrew poetry are familiar. We have first
parallelism of lines and thought, a form which lends itself to many
varieties. In addition we have accentual rhythm, such that the usual
lines have three stresses, although this number may change. Even in
English translation we can often recognize the underlying Hebrew
pattern. For example:

> I will bless the Lord at all times;
> his praises shall continually be in my mouth.
> My soul makes it boast in the Lord;
>   let the afflicted hear and be glad.
> O magnify the Lord with me
>   and let us exalt his name together!

(Ps. 34.1–3.)

The poetic forms of the Old Testament which reappear in the
New are also often distinguished under three heads according to the
traditions out of which they come: (1) the 'gnome': the aphorism
of the wisdom tradition of Israel, often found in highly patterned
and pungent form; (2) the 'oracle': inspired rhythmic warning,
promise, vision, curse, in the tradition of Old Testament prophecy;

[1] Ernst Fuchs, *Hermeneutik*, § 22, 'Das Lied', pp. 262–4.

(3) the 'psalm': liturgical prayer-poems in the tradition of the psalter. We find our best examples of the gnome and the oracle in the sayings of Jesus. Examples of the Christian use of the psalm, of course, are found in the Canticles of Luke.

But we also have texts in the New Testament that we can best speak of as 'hymns', or as 'odes'. These are poetic forms of a liturgical character going back to a syncretist tradition, and found especially in brief confessional formulas or longer mythological recitations.

The new voice of the Gospel, whether in Jesus himself or in the anonymous utterances of the Early Church, thus takes up and shapes to its own use traditional vehicles both biblical and Hellenistic, especially for worship but also for teaching and exhortation. The poetry of the Jewish Bible and the Jewish liturgy is used and new creations in their styles are added to it. In such cases the eschatological miracle of the Gospel is read into the old or shapes the new. Similarly the styles of Hellenistic paganism or of Hellenistic Judaism are adopted and adapted as vehicles for the Gospel.

It is well to remind ourselves at this point of how large a part poetry plays in the Jewish Scriptures and in later Jewish writings such as the Apocrypha and the Dead Sea Scrolls. Thus we remember that the oracles of the prophets were in most cases poems, phrased in a long tradition of declamatory or elegiac rhythm. The wisdom literature also is in poetic form, including almost all of the Book of Job. We think also, of course, of the Psalter. We further recall many particular poems and oracles that are found scattered through the narrative books of the Old Testament.

Equally significant is the fact that the poetic elements are often basic to the whole structure of Israel's religion and literature. Recitative sections of Exodus and Deuteronomy such as the song of Moses in the fifteenth chapter of Exodus, the blessing of Moses in ch. 33 of Deuteronomy, and certain Psalms and passages in the prophets are not only very ancient (at least in their substance) but represent, as it were, the oral core out of which the more elaborate prose narratives arose. Similarly in the New Testament, the rhythmic sayings of Jesus on the one hand, and the liturgical-poetic confessions of the old oral tradition of the Church, lie beneath and behind the prose of the Gospels and the Epistles. It is worth noting, moreover, that the two books of the Old Testament most often quoted in the New are books of poetry: Isaiah and the Psalter.

We have a good deal of information about the place of the Psalms

and other poetic legacies in the worship of the Jews in the time of
Jesus. We know, of course, that many of the Psalms were recited
with musical accompaniments in the Temple, especially at the great
feasts, as well as read in the synagogue. But there were other poetic
sections of the Old Testament, not in the Psalter, that had great
importance in Judaism. One was the ancient song of Moses and
Miriam to which we have referred, the paean of triumph over
Pharaoh and the Egyptians beginning:

> 'I will sing to the Lord, for he has triumphed gloriously;
> the horse and his rider he has thrown into the sea'
>
> (Ex. 15.1).

This ode was recited at the Jewish Passover, as it still is, and was
taken over by the Early Church and used as a fitting feature in the
service of baptism. At some time in the second century it was introduced into the Easter vigil service of the Christians.[1] Already the
Book of Revelation refers to it as it describes those who had gotten
the victory over the Beast and over his image, having the harps of
God in their hands:

> And they sing the song of Moses, the servant of God,
>   and the song of the Lamb, saying: Great and
> marvellous are thy works, Lord God Almighty (Rev. 15.2–3).

One of the things we have come to understand about the tableaux of
heavenly worship in the Apocalypse is that they reflect the forms of
Jewish temple worship, though they also have features of worship in
the first-century Church. It is therefore very likely that the Christians
of Ephesus, for example, took over the Red Sea paean from synagogue usage and gave it a place in their own prayers.[2] We can see
how appropriate to Christian worship were such passages of the Ode
as the following:

> thou hast led in thy steadfast love the people whom
>   thou hast redeemed,
> thou has guided them by thy strength to thy holy abode (v. 13).

---

[1] 'The Christians may have taken this usage over from the Jewish Passover
celebrations, but now the deliverance from the hand of Pharaoh became an image
of redemption in Christ: the crossing of the Red Sea appeared as a symbol of
baptism; and from the Song of Triumph of the Hebrews came the Pascal Hymn of
Thanksgiving of the redeemed, especially of those just baptized. It is for this reason
that an Easter sermon of Hippolytus of Rome closes with the words: "O, Lord,
give us the joy to sing the triumph-hymn of Moses!" '—H. Schneider, 'Die
biblischen Oden im christlichen Altertum', *Biblica* 30 (1949), p. 37.

[2] *Ibid.*, pp. 34–35.

There is evidence also that the Song of Hannah, the mother of Samuel, had a place of honour in the Jewish liturgy. The *Magnificat* belongs to the same pattern as this poem which evidently begins in the same way:

> My heart exults in the Lord;
> my strength is exalted in the Lord (I Sam. 2.1).

Other Old Testament poems that were specially cherished by both Jews and Christians were the Song of Deborah, the Psalm of Habukkuk, the Great Ode of Moses in Deuteronomy 32, Jonah's Song in the Belly of the Fish, the Song of the Three Children in the Fiery Furnace (a supplement to Daniel 3 in the Apocrypha), and others. The Jews used such poems in the synagogue prayers or as lyrical interludes between readings in formal Temple or synagogue worship. Later we find the Christians also using them.

The famous Greek Bible manuscript which we call the Codex Alexandrinus, has a whole collection of such hymns gathered together as a 'Book of Odes' at the end of the Psalter. It includes the poems mentioned and others, fourteen in all.

One of the interesting features of New Testament poetry on its Jewish side is that when one retraces its forms one is led back beyond the whole history of Israel's poetry to Canaanite[1] and Mesopotamian prototypes. The Christian songs in our Book of Revelation and the first two chapters of Luke have at least antecedents in very ancient 'pagan' chants. Some English hymns that we sing today are metrical transcriptions of Psalms in the King James Version, and these go back to the Hebrew Psalter of the Jewish Temple and before that to ancient Israel; and these have their prototypes in hymns sung to the Canaanite Baal or the Babylonian Marduk. Thus our contemporary Christian lyrics, laments and doxologies have a tacit diapason of the praises and prayers of ancient humanity. And yet there are changes not only in theme but in style.

The twenty-ninth Psalm, one of the most stunning and numinous of the Psalms has been taken over bodily from a Canaanite model.

> The voice of the Lord is upon the
>   waters;
> the God of glory thunders,
> the Lord, upon many waters.

[1] Cf. John Patton, *Canaanite Parallels in the Book of Psalms* (Baltimore 1944).

The voice of the Lord is powerful,
   the voice of the Lord is full of majesty.

The voice of the Lord breaks the cedars,
   the Lord breaks the cedars of Lebanon.

He makes Lebanon to skip like a calf,
   and Sirion like a young wild ox.

The voice of the Lord flashes forth flames of fire.
   The voice of the Lord shakes the wilderness,
   the Lord shakes the wilderness of Kadesh.

The voice of the Lord makes the oaks to whirl,
   and strips the forests bare;
   and in his temple all cry, 'Glory!'

The Lord sits enthroned over the flood;
   The Lord sits enthroned as king for ever. (Vv. 3–10.)

Here the original meaning of 'Lord' was Baal. The Hebrew poet has converted this nature paean by putting it in an Israelite envelope at the beginning and conclusion by reference to the 'name'—that is Jahweh—and to the 'people' that is, Israel, and to *shalom*, peace, that is the Hebrew benediction. More general influences of Canaanite poetry are found in metric forms especially of the earliest Hebrew compositions (1100–900 BC), including some quite intricate ones. We can only mention briefly recurring patterns in the Psalms which go back to Babylonian ritual, reflecting the experience of the king in his triumphant reign and in his ordeals of humiliation and lamentation, presented in the first person.

   We can return to this twenty-ninth Psalm to point out one major feature of biblical poetry, its liturgical character. In the King James Version, the second verse (part of the added Hebrew introduction) reads:

        Give unto the Lord the glory due unto his name;
        worship the Lord in the beauty of holiness.

The 'beauty of holiness' suggests modern religious sentiment and a private kind of devotion. But the RSV translates better the original Hebrew:

        Ascribe to the Lord the glory of his name;
        worship the Lord in holy array.

'Holy array' refers to the ritual ceremony of Temple worship. The Psalm is a cult hymn not a private prayer. This holds for most if not all the Psalms as it does for their prototypes in ancient Near-Eastern hymns. This has an important bearing on most New Testament poems. Even in the case of the famous Song of Deborah we can detect the process by which an ancient war ballad has been converted into what one scholar calls a 'liturgical canticle' for use at one of the older Israelite sanctuaries as part of a cycle of *res gestae*, or heroic rehearsals of the tribes.[1] The Song of Moses in Exodus 15 similarly has marks of original antiphonal composition somewhat blurred now in its re-editing for later use in Solomon's Temple.[2]

We shall return to other aspects of Hebrew poetry, but we would make one observation at this point. The speech-art and rhythmic verse of the Bible, whether in the Psalter, the prophets or the wisdom literature, take up non-biblical or as we can say universal material into it. We have a wedding of general human experience with revelation. This suggests that all the Christian arts to this day must be built on human nature and its Adamic vitalities and creativity. The Christian arts should not be hot-house products confined to the shrine and isolated from the world. The idiom of Christian poetry and song should not be that of a peculiar language of Zion or a passionless song of angels. *Paradise Lost* was the work not only of a Puritan but also of a Renaissance man. Bach took up secular motifs into his Masses. The Negro spirituals have their force and poignancy because not only the life of the slave but ancient rhythms of African ceremonies are transmuted into faith. Faith grows bright because it is fed by the fuel of generic mortal experience.

III

Let us turn to the poetry of Palestinian Judaism in the time of Christ. We have recognized that the poetry of the past, whether of Psalmist, prophet or wise man, continued to be used in Jewish life both public and private. But how far was poetry still a living art? Were new poems being written? What is the bridge from Jewish to Christian poetry? We might suppose that the great vitality of Pharisaism in its concern with the law in its legal and social aspects would have displaced creative types of expression. For one thing,

[1] J. Blenkinsopp, 'Ballad Style and Psalm Style in the Song of Deborah', *Biblica* 42/1 (1961), pp. 61–76.
[2] *Ibid.*, p. 63.

however, the scribes were also active on the haggadic side of the
Jewish tradition—its saga—and much imagination and delight went
into this elaboration of the narrative side of the Scripture. From the
Pharisees had recently come, moreover, the Psalms of Solomon in the
tradition of the Psalter, and such poems as we find in Tobit, ch. 13.
In the second century BC a lover of the law had written the fifty
chapters of Ecclesiasticus in the wisdom tradition, and we have other
pieces like the Song of the Three Holy Children added to Daniel.
We come closer home now with important new evidence of an
Aramaic poetry being written in the period of Christ—a topic to
which we shall return. In listing poetry written by the Jews in this
period we should also have in mind the more Hellenized kind found
in the Book of Wisdom and farther afield in the Jewish Sibyllines.

But it is in apocalyptic and sectarian groups that we find our
fullest documentation of the continuation of Hebrew poetry, both in
the prophetic and in the Psalter tradition. Here our attention is
drawn to the Dead Sea Scrolls particularly. Their library included
the striking collection of Thanksgiving Hymns, the *Hodayot*, found in
the first cave. But other writings, including the Manual of Discipline
and the War Scroll include poetic sections. The hymn in the Manual
suggests how important a place the song of praise had in the life of
these Essenes. The theme of this psalm is the praise of God's order
for men and for nature, for the cycles of the world and of the seasons.
By such songs these children of the light identified themselves
mystically with the eternal covenant and ordinances of God who
ruled over the dawn and the evening and also over the ways of men.[1]

> I will sing with knowledge,
> and all my music shall be for glory of God;
> my lyre and harp shall be for his holy fixed order,
> and the flute of my lips I will raise
> in his just circle.
>
> With the coming of day and night
> I will enter the covenant of God;
> and with the outgoing of evening and morning
> I will speak his decrees;
> and while they exist I will set my limit
> so that I may not turn back.[2]

---

[1] A. Dupont-Sommer, *Les écrits esséniens découverts près de la mer morte* (Paris
1959), pp. 112–13.

[2] Translation: Millar Burrows, *The Dead Sea Scrolls* (New York 1955), p. 385.

Dupont-Sommer translates these two last lines as follows:

> while they exist, I will take up my station
> there inalterably.

This scholar comments on the hymn as follows: 'In the presence of the unchangeable laws which rule the courses of the stars, the believer communes with all his soul in the eternal and marvellous incorruptibility of the celestial world. This astral mysticism . . . was widely prevalent in the Hellenistic period.'[1]

The Hymn Scroll itself represents a particular type of psalm such as we meet in the Psalter, although the genre has become mixed, a genre entitled, 'the thanksgiving poem of the individual'. Our manuscript contains forty psalms in whole or in part, and it is evident that they were much used, since parts of at least six other copies have been found. As Professor Frank M. Cross, Jr, has noted, these and other Jewish psalms of the Maccabean period and later have gone through a considerable formal development. Sapiential elements have influenced the style. We see a breakdown in the older patterns of symmetry. The closest parallels to these are to be found in the apocalyptic hymns of the Apocrypha and of the New Testament.[2] The Thanksgiving Hymns while evidencing real individual vitality are heavily dependent upon the writings of the Old Testament, not only the Psalter but the prophets and the Book of Lamentations.

To put these psalms into the context of our discussion, we make one or two observations. As genuinely poignant prayers the dialogue aspect which we have found so important is undoubtedly present. Nevertheless, expression is somewhat strained and the style somewhat diluted by gratuitous and derivative expansions. The special sectarian dogma, if we may call it that, acts as a weight on the amplitude of utterance, and we often feel that we are in the presence of conventional written texts rather than free poems that take wing in oral address. Again, with respect to the essential narrative or story substance which we have found so essential for biblical rhetoric: there

---

[1] *Ibid.*, footnote 1, p. 14.
[2] Frank Moore Cross, Jr, *The Ancient Library of Qumran* (New York 1958), pp. 122–3. See also Charles F. Kraft, who remarks of the variety of metrical structure that it 'seems to amount almost to metrical chaos'; and of parallelism, 'rarely does this appear in more than a few lines of exact and simple synonymous, antithetic or synthetic parallelism'—'Poetical Structure of the Qumran Thanksgiving Psalms', *Biblical Research* 2 (1957), p. 18.

is surprisingly little concrete recital of the way of God with man and
with Israel in the past. Only a narrow priestly strand of the heritage,
set in a somewhat abstract-mystical predestination scheme, is invoked. We have the song of an apocalyptic-priestly community. The
faith of the author is esoteric, indeed one of his pledges is that he will
hide the secret revelation. The true root of the religion here and his
lyric expression is found in such a passage as this:

> A light is in my heart from his marvellous mysteries;
> my eye has gazed on that which is eternal. (XI, 3.)

One point at which the poetry of the Hodayot Scroll comes alive
is where the poet dwells upon the mystery precisely of the gift of
inspired chant, the creative miracle of language, of numbers, and of
harmony.

> Thou didst create breath with the tongue;
> thou knewest its words and didst establish the fruit of the lips
> before they existed.
> Thou didst place words on a line,
> and the utterance of the breath of the lips in measure;
> thou didst bring forth *sounds according to their mysterious laws*
> and the *emissions of breathings according to their harmony.*
> to make known thy glory. . . .
> I, 27–30 (Burrows, p. 401; italics represent the version at these
> points of Dupont-Sommer, p. 219).

We see here a somewhat sophisticated awareness of poetic creation.
Dupont-Sommer reminds us of the Pythagorean interest in numbers
and in cosmic harmony. But the vitality of the expression of the
Qumran poet is related to the theme of his oracles, and to his sense
that God's inspired chant constitutes a revelation powerful in the
life of the saints and the world.

> [For] thou has opened a [fountain] in the mouth of thy servant
> and on his tongue thou hast engraven [thy precepts] according to
>   a measure
> [that he might] proclaim them to the creature, thanks to his
>   understanding,
> and that he might serve as an interpreter in these matters for
>   that which is dust [like myself].
> And thou hast opened [his fountain]
> to rebuke the creature of clay for his doings . . .
> and to open up the ordinances of truth . . .
> [to him] who announces good news in the time of thy favour,

proclaiming the good news to the humble according to the abundance of mercy
and giving them to drink at the fountain of thy holiness.

XVIII. 10–15 (Dupont-Sommer).[1]

It is evident that the poetry as a whole suffers from diffuseness and derivativeness.[2] Abstractions play too large a part. We hear repeatedly of wickedness and its synonyms: perversity, impiety, vanity, rebellion, folly, idolatry, iniquity and their opposites, but without concrete examples and plastic eloquence. Exceptions are, however, to be found. There are occasional concrete metaphors or similes from earlier Scripture; some of which are carried out with independent resourcefulness like that of the conflagration that melts the foundation of the hills and reaches to Sheol itself (XVII, 13; III, 29–32); the pangs of childbirth (III, 7 ff.); the sailors in a foundering ship (III, 6, 13–16; VI, 22–24; VII, 19); the city whose foundations are shaken or steadfast (III, 7, 13; VI, 25–28). Many lesser figures help to redeem the didactic conventionality: the bird chased from its nest (IV, 9); the persecutors pictured as lions (V, 6–14); the Messianic Branch (VIII, 6, 10; VI, 15–18; VII, 19); the army of heaven (III, 34–35; cf. XVIII, 23; III, 22–23); the storehouses or treasuries of nature: hail, rain, lightning, etc. (I, 12–13).

We should add one word about the seven or more martial hymns or hymnic prayers found in the War Scroll. At one point here (XV, 5), Dupont-Sommer sees it probable that the collection of Thanksgiving Psalms was read as a whole by the chief priest in the course of the great Armaggedon preparations described.[3] This is unlikely. The character of the poetry in this Scroll is appreciably different. They are more like the Old Testament Psalter in the large place given to the actual history of Israel, the role of the patriarchs, the deliverance from Egypt and the entrance into the promised land.

In the Hymn Scroll, on the other hand, the works and ordinances of God are set in a cosmic perspective and deal with creation and eternal decrees. The calendar of Jewish worship is taken up into an eternal metaphysical setting and its relation to the historical experi-

---

[1] Cf. VIII, 4, 'For thou hast set me as a fountain of streams in a dry place'; VIII, 16, 'And thou, O God, hast put in my mouth, as it were, an autumn rain for all the sons of men, and a spring of living waters that will not fail.'

[2] 'The phraseology of the author is sometimes imperfect and confused as in other writings of Qumran'—J. P. M. van der Ploeg (apropos 1QM, XIII, 7–16), Le Rouleau de la guerre (Leiden 1959), p. 152.

[3] Dupont-Sommer, p. 214.

ence of Israel is to that extent evaporated. It agrees with this that behind the Thanksgiving Scroll we hear a very individual author. God reveals himself here not so much in the long history of Israel and its actual covenants as in the private vision of this particular psalmist.[1] There is one basic covenant, that of the Sect, and this overlaps with the one cosmic covenant God had made with his creation and all flesh before time began. The Qumran community must have had in it a tension between concern with the Old Testament heritage, especially priestly, and concern with the new wisdom of revelation which certainly had a syncretist character. The former emphasis manifest in the War Scroll gives us a poetry more like the Book of Psalms. The latter emphasis gives us a poetry of a more modern individualistic kind.[2] In the Christian Church we find a similar distinction between poetry of biblical Jewish roots and poetry shaped by syncretist and even gnostic patterns. Among both Essenes and Christians when the Old Testament tradition is followed the poetry is marked as in the Psalter, by recitation of God's acts and promises, especially by synonymous and cumulative parallelism; while the new mystery tradition discloses itself especially in sharply antithetical parallelism, based on a world divided between light and darkness.

IV

We have looked at the Jewish background of early Christian poetry. Let us turn now directly to the New Testament. There are two texts that immediately come to mind. The first is taken from the letter to the Colossians:

> Let the word of Christ dwell in you richly, as you teach and admonish one another in all wisdom, and as you sing psalms (*psalmois*) and hymns (*hymnois*) and spiritual songs (*ōdais pneumatikais*) with thankfulness in your hearts to God (3.16).

Evidently the Church of Paul's time had its own Christian poems as well as those taken over from Judaism. The term 'psalm' here need not mean only those of David. The Greek terms translated 'hymns'

[1] Cf. M. Mansoor, citing Bardtke: there is 'no mention in the Hodayot or elsewhere in the scrolls of the acts of deliverance of Israel, so frequently recounted in the Old Testament, such as the Exodus, the crossing of the Red Sea and the conquest of Canaan. Only the acts of creation are mentioned', *The Thanksgiving Hymns* (Leiden 1961), p. 27. But in the War Scroll the deliverance at the Red Sea *is* mentioned (XI, 9–10) and there are frequent references to the choice of Israel and its basic historical covenant.

[2] Note the characterization of the Hodayot by Theodore Gaster, 'Especially noteworthy is the prevalence in these hymns of the vocabulary which Evelyn

and 'spiritual songs' suggest a great variety of poetic resource.[1] Our second text is taken from the First Epistle to the Corinthians. Here we have details on an early Christian service.

> What then, brethren? When you come together, each one has a hymn (*psalmon*), a lesson, a revelation (*apocalypsin*), a tongue (*glōssan*), or an interpretation (14.26).

In a meeting of this kind it is clear that creative lyrical expression had its place. Certainly this would be true of those who contributed a 'hymn'; it would no doubt also be true of those who voice a 'revelation' or oracle. Speaking with tongues was certainly rhythmic and we in our day would be the last to insist that poetry must be intelligible! The early Christian meetings, judged by such texts as these, were evidently by no means dull. We can surmise that there must have been a good deal of very 'modern' poetry and free verse in their exchanges. If we had been present we would probably have found a wide range of chanting and declamation ranging from equivalents of our litanies, spirituals and *Te Deums* to uninhibited hallelujahs and religious enthusiasm.[2]

Underhill and others have recognized as the standard and characteristic idiom of mystical experience. There is the same harping on the wilderness of isolation; the same reference to the "ascent" to God and to the "height of eternal things"; the same metaphor (particularly in Hymn No. 5) of the New Birth and the "travail of the world"; the same intensive apprehension of Divine providence, communion and "enlightenment"; and the same sense of nursing a precious secret against the day of revelation. Apprehension of these notes is of the essence in understanding the spirit of the hymns in particular and of the Brotherhood in general.' *The Scriptures of the Dead Sea Sect* (London 1957), p. 120.

[1] Hippolytus writing about AD 200 speaks of psalms and odes of the brethren which were composed by believers from the beginning. For the terminology see Heinrich Schneider, 'Die biblische Oden im christlichen Altertum', *Biblica* 30 (1949), pp. 28–65; 239–72; 433–52; 479–500; and G. Delling, *op. cit.*, pp. 86–87.

[2] The effectiveness of popular group songs, often improvised, in a situation calling for endurance has been recently demonstrated among the Negroes in the desegregation sit-ins and demonstrations. In an article in the *New York Times*, August 20, 1962, entitled, 'Songs a Weapon in Rights Battle', by Robert Shelton, it is noted that 'spirituals, hymns and gospel songs help bolster the morale of integrationists and disarm the hostility of segregationists. . . . The songs, new and old, are used at mass meetings, demonstrations, prayer vigils, on Freedom Rides, in jails and before sit-ins.' Martin Luther King is cited as follows: 'The freedom songs are playing a strong and vital role in our struggle. They give the people new courage and a sense of unity.' An official of the NAACP, speaking of an organizational meeting in Georgia, observes: 'The people were cold with fear. Music did what prayer and speeches could not do in breaking the ice.' A biblical analogy is evoked in a report of the Albany Police Chief that 'while booking more than 260 persons in a mass arrest, the jail guards were singing and humming songs along with the prisoners'.

But it was not only in the stated meetings of the community that poetry had its place. Hymns and psalms were a part of private and family devotion. We do not need to look far for evidence of this. The account in the Book of Acts of the imprisonment of Paul and his companions at Philippi includes the following:

> But about midnight Paul and Silas were praying and singing hymns (*hymnoun*) to God . . . and suddenly there was a great earthquake, so that the foundations of the prison were shaken (16.25–26).

We can be quite sure that the Psalter was used in family worship among the Christians, particularly in connection with table prayers. Evidence for this is found on the one hand in what we know about Jewish family practice in this period—especially at the end of the Sabbath and at the Passover—and also in what the Church Fathers tell us.[1]

Since the *Magnificat* in the first chapter of Luke is the best known of our New Testament hymns we may well pause to consider it. Scholars in the past (Harnack, Gunkel, Torrey) have recognized that an eschatological poem in Hebrew or Aramaic underlies our Greek text. They have also recognized here a familiar Jewish pattern. Such psalms begin with the formula, 'let us praise God, because so and so.' In other words: 'My soul doth magnify the Lord . . . for.' The song of Hannah in I Sam. 2.1–10 begins similarly: 'My heart exults in the Lord . . . because I rejoice in thy salvation.' There then follows a series of couplets listing the great acts of God in a tense indicating completed action; but these actions are also understood in an eschatological sense, for they refer to judgment day yet to come. We can illustrate from the *Magnificat*:

> He has shown strength with his arm,
> he has scattered the proud in the imagination of their hearts,
> he has put down the mighty from their thrones,
> and exalted those of low degree. . . .

The pattern then comes to an end with a single concluding verse

[1] Lucetta Mowry, *Poetry in the Synoptic Gospels and Revelation*, unpublished MS (Yale Doctoral Dissertation), pp. 94–96, 270, citing Tertullian, *Ad Uxor.* 28. She also notes that Tobit 3.1–6 puts us on the track of family prayers on the occasion of a death in the family. The prayer here of Tobit for release suggests the proper background for the *Nunc Dimittis*, Luke 2.29–32. Cf. E. J. Goodspeed, *Problems in New Testament Translation* (Chicago 1945), pp. 77–79: 'Now, Master, you will let your slave go free', Luke 2.29. The basic idea here is the emancipation, not the discharge, of a bondservant.

which generalizes the theme, in this case invoking the promises to the fathers:

> He has helped his servant Israel,
> in remembrance of his mercy,
> as he spoke to our fathers,
> to Abraham and to his posterity for ever.

In the Old Testament, praise-poems of this kind may at some time be connected with a personal hero or heroine by certain adaptations.[1] The *Magnificat*, in substance a very old poem, has thus been found an appropriate expression for Mary and the adaptation has been carried out especially by the addition of verse 48:

> For he has regarded the low estate of his handmaiden.
> For behold, henceforth all generations will call me blessed.[2]

As we reconstruct the original Semitic form of this Canticle it could have been composed by either a Jewish or a Christian poet. Retroversion into Aramaic or Hebrew brings to light the familiar patterns of accentual rhythm in the couplets, three stresses matching three.[3] The first Christians must have used more of such hymns of an Old Testament kind than we find cited in our New Testament.

Before we examine further the poetry of the Early Church let us consider poetic elements in the sayings of Jesus himself. Since he spoke in Aramaic it is relevant to inquire what evidence we may have for Aramaic poetic style in this period. The most recent work on this subject has been done by Matthew Black of St Andrews.[4] Our very limited examples of Aramaic writing of this period have recently been greatly increased. A copy of the Jerusalem Targum of the whole Pentateuch (Cod. Neofiti I) was identified by a Spanish scholar in Barcelona in 1956. One of Black's remarks about this Targum bears on our present interest.

> One of the most important features of this Targum for our purpose is that within the free paraphrase there have survived a number of old

---

[1] Thus with Jonah, verse 1 in Jonah 2.1–9; with Hannah, verse 1 in I Sam. 2.1–10; with Habakkuk, verse 1 in Hab. 3.1–19.

[2] Note also the addition of 'for me' in verse 49. Harnack and others have seen the poem as first attributed to Elizabeth as, indeed, some early manuscripts indicate.

[3] L. Mowry, *op. cit.*, pp. 278–86. C. C. Torrey sees a basic 3/2 metre in the Aramaic; in *Studies in Early Christianity*, ed. S. J. Case, pp. 298–300.

[4] 'The Recovery of the Language of Jesus', *NTS* 3 (1957), pp. 305–13. Also, *An Aramaic Approach to the Gospels and Acts*, 2nd ed., Oxford 1957.

liturgical hymns, original Aramaic compositions often modelled on a theme or text from Scripture, and probably first composed for recitation, on special occasions such as the Festivals, in the Synagogue. They come next to the psalms, hymns and prophetic utterances of the Hebrew Old Testament as literary parallels to the hymns, prayers and poetic (and prophetic) teaching of Christ; and they are composed in free, idiomatic Palestinian Aramaic.[1]

Another large addition to our knowledge of the language of Jesus is the Scroll found in the Cave I and named, 'A Genesis Apocryphon'. This text with its 22 columns is in Aramaic. Here, too, Black finds poetic passages such as the description of Sarah's beauty. Using all such Aramaic materials Black has sought to identify Aramaic poetry wherever it may lie behind the Greek of our Gospels. He thus carries further the older studies made by C. S. Burney and others. By retroversion of the Greek into Aramaic he finds the typical features of poetry in the latter tongue—parallelism, assonance, word-play, etc.—in Luke's hymns, in sayings of the Baptist (both in the Synoptics and in John), but especially in the sayings of Jesus. To quote:

> Jesus did not commit anything to writing, but by His use of poetic form and language, He insured that His sayings would not be forgotten. The impression they make in Aramaic is of carefully premeditated and studied deliverances; we have to do with prophetic utterances of the style and grandeur of Isaiah, cast in a medium which can express in appropriate and modulated sound the underlying beauty of the sentiment or the passion out of which the thought arose.[2]

There is no question as to the presence of underlying Aramaic poetic forms in much of the teaching and we are grateful to Black for his careful study of its features. We are not persuaded, however, that Jesus' sayings were 'studied' in this sense, nor given particular form for mnemonic purposes. We should, moreover, find some way of doing justice to the speech of Jesus without using modern idealistic categories ('the beauty of the sentiment'), and without distinguishing the 'medium' from the 'thought'.

Miss Lucetta Mowry has studied the various types of Hebrew poetry and examined the Gospels against this background. She identifies the three different poetic types: the gnome of the wise man,

[1] *NTS* 3 (1957), p. 306. Black is speaking of the Palestine Targum tradition in general, but the new complete MS greatly supplements our acquaintance with it.

[2] *An Aramaic Approach to the Gospels*, 2nd ed., p. 142.

the oracle of the prophet, and the psalm. Among the Jews sub-types and mixed types had developed. Miss Mowry tests the Gospel material by rather strict criteria. On this basis she cannot accept the all too generous conclusions of Burney and others. She finds only twenty sayings of Jesus that can be called poetry, all in the Synoptic Gospels. Seventeen of these belong to the gnome category; two to that of prophetic oracle; and one, the Lord's Prayer, falls into a type we occasionally meet in the Psalter, that of a sequence of petitions.

To recover some due sense of the power of Jesus' utterance we must refer back to passages in the prophets:

> Behold I will make my words in thy mouth fire,
> And the people wood, and it shall devour them.
>
> Is not my word like a fire, saith the Lord;
> And like a hammer that breaketh the rock in pieces?
>
> (Jer. 5.14; 23.29.)

The words of Jesus were spoken with this kind of power. Inevitably many of them took on the character of rhythmic proclamation and strophe. His utterances could be either austere or gentle, but in either case they came from the depths. The Bible speaks of the 'fruit of the lips', and this metaphor suggests a wondrous blossoming and bearing of fruit indeed.

v

When we look beyond the Synoptic Gospels we find rhythmic passages in the early Christian writings which are of great interest. We can call most of these texts 'poetry' if we are willing to include not only those which are evidently hymns but also those of a recitational character. The term 'liturgical' covers both of these. Such citations of poetic praise or confession appear especially in the Epistles and their dense style stands out like crystal in its matrix, to use a comparison of Ethelbert Stauffer. In such cases we can usually tell the difference between poetry and heightened prose. Paul's hymn to love in I Corinthians is rhythmic indeed, but we would not count it as poetry. In the Revised Standard Version some of the material of which we are speaking is printed as poetry and some not. Of the sections so printed the three following may be cited. They are no doubt citations of ancient Christian liturgical hymns whose archaic power lifts them out of their contexts like trumpet blasts.

> Awake, O sleeper, and arise from the dead,
> and Christ shall give you light.
>
> (Eph. 5.14.)

> He was manifested in the flesh,
> acknowledged in the Spirit,
>   seen by angels,
> preached among the nations,
> believed on in the world,
>   taken up in glory.
>
> (I Tim. 3.16.)

> If we have died with him, we shall also live with him;
> if we endure, we shall also reign with him;
> if we deny him, he also will deny us;
> if we are faithless, he remains faithful. . . .
>
> (II Tim. 2.11b–13a.)

Such fragments of poetry in the New Testament can be supplemented from those found in the letters of Ignatius and in other noncanonical writings. They prepare us for the report made by Pliny in his famous letter to Trajan early in the second century. He tells us that the Christians in his province in Asia Minor arose before dawn for their meetings and in their worship sang a hymn to Christ as to a god:

> carmen Christo quasi deo dicere soliti
>
> (*Ep.* X, 96, 7).

Let us return to the first of the fragments quoted above, that from the fifth chapter of Ephesians. We cite the translation found in the New English Bible:

> Awake, sleeper,
> Rise from the dead,
> And Christ will shine upon you.

Two features of the context are of interest. The lines are introduced by the words, 'Therefore it is said,' showing that we have before us a familiar utterance. The source of the utterance is no doubt defined four verses below: 'addressing one another in psalms and hymns and spiritual songs, singing and making melody to the Lord with all your heart' (5.19). Another feature of the context is the moral charge of the preceding section, 'walk in love' (v. 2), modulated to 'walk as children of light' (v. 8), as the sins envisaged move from wrath and anger to debauchery and shame. But the awaking from sleep in question no doubt is associated with baptism which could be seen as illumination: 'Christ will shine upon you.' Our hymn is probably an early baptismal text, relevant to a moral appeal to the faithful reminding them of their initial transformation as suggested at the beginning of this section of Ephesians: 'Put off your old nature . . . and put on the new nature' (4.22–24).

The appropriateness of the poem for baptism is reinforced if we complete it as Clement of Alexandria does by a supplement which may well be original.[1]

> Awake, sleeper,
> Rise from the dead,
> And Christ will shine upon you:
> The Sun of the Resurrection,
> He who was born before the dawn,
> Whose beams give life.

In any case we have here a kind of rhetoric which stands out by its style and density like sapphires in clay. Many of these early oral fragments have the impact of ramshorns in their concentration, imagery and hyperbole.

> Arise from the dead!

One is reminded of the legendary cry of a French officer in an emergency in the Battle of Verdun in 1917 when the enemy was breaking into the position and his entire platoon had been killed by the preceding barrage:

> Debout les morts!

This kind of paradox in speech is at home in the world of faith and miracle. It is like the words of Jesus to Peter telling him to walk on the water. Or it is like his words to the man with the withered arm: 'Stretch forth thy hand!' More relevant to our present hymn is the command of Christ at the grave of Lazarus: 'Lazarus, come forth!' So,

> Awake, sleeper,
> Rise from the dead!

Christian speech can have this kind of sublime non-sense because it arises from those depths where the world is still fluid and where all our usual categories are in question.

---

[1] *Protrepticus* IX, 84 [Loeb, p. 186].

This hymn has its background not in the more typical Jewish styles but in Hellenistic and Gnostic imagery. Many religious groups of this time saw salvation as a matter of being roused from sleep or awakened from ignorance or sobered up from drunkenness. Man was under an evil spell of forgetfulness and illusion. Hence the figures of awakening, coming to oneself, casting off the darkness, emerging from a cave or pit. The early Christians used these categories. Christ is the Light who awakens from sleep and the Sun of the Resurrection who awakens from death; and the natural context is that of baptism. But this hymn would also fit into the situation described by Pliny in his letter to Trajan: 'The Christians arise before dawn and sing a hymn to Christ as a God.' What more suitable at this hour than to voice the appeal of our hymn to Christ, especially with its sequel:

> The Sun of Resurrection,
> He who was born before the dawn,
> Whose beams give life?

Of particular interest among the poetic sections identified in the New Testament is the striking early confession of Christ cited by Paul in his letter to the Philippians, 2.6–11 to support his theme of lowliness of mind. This strophic poem tells how Christ, though in the form of God, emptied himself and was obedient to death, and was then exalted by God and given a name which is above every name, that of Lord, *kyrios*. The original source may have been in the Aramaic tongue but its mythical background is evidently that of popular Hellenistic syncretism.[1] Ernst Lohmeyer notes of this poem, which he calls a Christian chorale, that it is not a Psalm in the usual sense, since it is not an expression of the subjective experience of the heart and the soul but sets forth a world-transaction. Many of the poems we are concerned with here similarly deal not with the feelings of the worshippers as in the case of the visionary transports of Gnostic meditations but with the fate of the world.

Scholars are also widely convinced that the prologue of the Gospel of John represents the re-editing of a Hellenistic poem on the Logos, in all likelihood Jewish-Hellenistic. Citations or traces of such

---

[1] E. Lohmeyer, *Kyrios Jesus; Eine Untersuchung zur Phil.* 2, 5–11, 1927–8; R. Bultmann, in *Coniectanea Neotestamentica* 11 (1947), pp. 1–14, especially p. 6; G. Bornkamm, 'Zum Verstaendnis des Christus-Hymnus, Phil. 2.6–11', *Studien zur Antike und Christentum* (Munich 1959), pp. 177–87; E. Käsemann, *ZTK* 47 (1950), 34 f.

theological poetry and recitation appear clearly in I Peter,[1] Hebrews,[2] and Colossians. The background for their vocabulary and rhetoric is found in such different writings as those of the Odes of Solomon, early Christian apocrypha, Ignatius, and Gnostic material of various kinds.

We can pursue this question of the background of such rhythmic texts by looking at a passage in the Epistle to the Colossians. We recall that it is in Col. 3.16 that we find the familiar reference to 'psalms and hymns and spiritual songs'. One such poem is preserved for us, though with some supplementation, in chapter I, verses 15 to 20. It is a mystical-philosophical recitation of the kind favoured by various theosophists of the time both Jewish and pagan. Ernst Käsemann believes that we have here a pagan text retouched by a Christian hand.[3] He reconstitutes the original poem as follows, in two stanzas:

> He is the image of the invisible God,
> the first-born of all creation;
> for in him all things were created.
> He is before all things,
> and in him all things hold together.
>
> He is the head of the body,
> he is the beginning,
> the first-born from the dead,
> that in everything he might be pre-eminent,
> that in him all things might be reconstituted
> in heaven and on earth.

Here we have in the first strophe the praise of the primal Man or Gnostic Saviour through whom all things were made, who, in the second strophe conquers death for all and reorders the 'body', that is the *plērōma* or universe. All this well fits into the pagan myth of the Gnostic redeemer. But in the form in which we have it in Colossians the hymn has been applied to Christ and references are introduced in the passage or its context to his Kingdom, to the forgiveness of sins, to the Church now seen as the 'body' and to the Cross. Thus the pagan mythological poem has been converted into a Christian

---

[1] See especially M. E. Boismard, *Quatre hymnes baptismales dans la première épître de Pierre* (Paris: Editions du Cerf 1961).

[2] Cf. G. Bornkamm, 'Homologia: Das Bekenntnis im Hebraerbrief', *op. cit.*, pp. 188–204.

[3] 'Eine urchristliche Taufliturgie', *Exegetische Versuche und Besinnungen*, Erster Band (Göttingen 1960), pp. 34–51 [ET to appear in *Exegetical Essays*].

baptismal confession. As Käsemann writes, the deliverance from the powers of darkness, and the transfer over into the kingdom of the Son of God's love actually takes place in the act of baptism.[1] The new status effected by the sacrament is spoken of in the twelfth verse as the 'inheritance of the saints in light'. Their 'lot' in the 'inheritance' picks up the theme of the Promised Land of the Old Testament but here takes on the meaning of Paradise itself. Even Judaism understood the redemption from Egypt as a new creation.[2]

It is evident that the Christians wrote or revised pagan hymns in the hieratic style of the time. In such liturgical material often God himself speaks in the first person. In the Gospel of John we find this style carried over.

> I know whence I have come
> and whither I am going,
> but you do not know whence I come
> or whither I am going.
>
> (8.14.)

> You know neither me nor my Father;
> If you knew me you would know my Father also.
>
> (8.19.)

> You are from below,
> I am from above;
> You are of this world,
> I am not of this world.
>
> (8.23.)

To suggest the background of this kind of early Christian poem I cite a model of Gnostic revelation-oracle as it is provided for us by Heinz Becker on the basis of many examples.

[1] *Ibid.*, p. 44.

[2] James M. Robinson has restored the text seen as a Christian liturgical 'hymn' in the following way. Here the clauses in the second stanza (redemption) correspond line for line with those in the first (creation):

Who is the image of the invisible God, The first-born of all creation	Who is the beginning, The first-born from the dead;
For in him were created all things in heaven and earth [And] all things [are] through him, and to him [have been created].	For in him [dwells] all the fulness [of deity (bodily)], And through him [he reconciled] all things to him.
And he himself is before all things, And all things in him have come together.	And he himself is the head of the body, That he might in all things himself be pre-eminent.

'A Formal Analysis of Colossians 1.15–20', *JBL* 76/4 (December 1957), p. 286.

I am the Revealer who am come from heaven.
I am of God,
you are of the world.
God is light,
the world is darkness.
I proclaim to you redemption from the world.
Leave the darkness,
Draw near to the light.
Abandon the works of the world
and do the deeds of God.
He who hearkens to me will look upon the light;
he who hearkens not to me will sink in the darkness.[1]

If one examines the Hellenistic hymns upon which this model is based one notes four features. First we have the oracular self-identification of the Revealer-Redeemer: 'I am so and so.' Compare, 'I am the Good Shepherd', or, 'I am Alpha and Omega'. These are sometimes found in the second person, 'Thou art, etc.' An example in the third person appears in Ignatius's epistle to the Ephesians:

> There is one Physician, who is both flesh and spirit, born and yet not born, who is God in man, true life in death, both of Mary and of God, first passible and then impassible, Jesus Christ our Lord (7.2).

In the second place we have the proclamation of the great cosmic turning-point: the Redeemer has been exalted and enthroned far above all rule and authority and power and dominion, and above every name that is named (Eph. 1.20–21; cf. 'I have overcome the world').[2] Thirdly, we have the call or invitation to all beings: 'Come unto me', or 'The Bride says, Come', or 'Awaken from sleep', or 'Arouse yourselves from drunkenness.' Finally, there is the promise of felicity, of heavenly mansions, of 'the place which is their due', i.e. that of the children of God.[3] In the Christian hymns of the New Testament and the early Fathers such aspects of the world-drama of salvation are echoed. From the point of view of meaningful communication we can see that current popular vehicles were employed both in the sense of rhetoric and of mythological symbolism.

---

[1] *Die Reden des Johannesevangeliums und der Stil der gnostischen Offenbarungsrede*, p. 57.
[2] Ignatius's letter to the Ephesians again affords us an illustration:
   A star shone in heaven beyond all the other stars. . . .
   By this all magic was dissolved
   and every bond of wickedness vanished away,
   Ignorance was removed,
   and the old kingdom was destroyed. (19.2f.)
[3] Polycarp, *Ad Phil.* 9.2; I Clem. 5.4.

There is one writing in the New Testament where it has not been commonly recognized that we have verse-forms, and this is the First Epistle of John. If one reads this letter with attention to its style one is struck by recurrent features of balanced phrasing. We may note first a number of examples which we would hardly admit as poetry. We come upon one instance immediately in the opening verse:

> That which was from the beginning,
>   which we have heard,
>   which we have seen with our eyes,
>   which we have looked upon
>   and touched with our hands.

This we would characterize as rhetorical prose. Similarly, when we come to the passage, twice-repeated, which runs:

> I am writing to you, little children . . .
> I am writing to you, fathers . . .
> I am writing to you, young men . . . (2.12–14).

Here, also, we have only stylized prose.

In the second and third verses of chapter 4 we have a kind of catechetical formula in antithetic parallelism:

> every spirit which confesses that Jesus Christ
>   has come in the flesh
> is of God,
> and every spirit which does not confess Jesus
> is not of God (4.2–3).

This is surely expositional rather than lyric. It is true that we do have confessions in lyrical or hymnic form in the Epistles, but their tenor is different.

Another example of balanced saying to set aside is the following:

> every one who loves the parent
> loves the child (5.1).

This is in all likelihood an instance of a popular aphorism taken from current usage. Such sayings are often in couplet form, in any language. Other examples can be found in the New Testament. Jesus, no doubt, cites such an adage of the streets when he says:

> to him who has will more be given;
> and from him who has not, even what he has will
>   be taken away (Mark 4.25).

But the peculiar verse-pattern in I John that we have in mind is different from any of these above. Nor does it resemble the Hebraic style of poetry which we find in the Old Testament. Rather, it represents a Hellenistic type as we might expect in this writing. We strike this element or source used in the epistle when we come to the fifth verse of the first chapter:

> God is light
> and in him there is no darkness at all.

This is adversative parallelism. But its most distinctive character appears when we find a series of triple lines balanced against each other:

> He who says he is in the light
> and hates his brother
> is in the darkness still.
>
> He who loves his brother
> abides in the light,
> and in it there are no pitfalls.
>
> But he who hates his brother
> is in the darkness
> and walks in the darkness (2.9–11).

To take an example from the fourth chapter:

> They are of the world,
> therefore what they saw is of the world,
> and the world listens to them.
>
> We are of God:
> Whoever knows God listens to us,
>
> and he who is not of God
> does not listen to us (4.5–6).

These are enough evidence to suggest that this letter rests on a poetic source which it continually cites, and to which the writer adds his own comments and applications. Rudolf Bultmann finds such a source not only here but also through parts of the Gospel of John. If this material is not poetry in the sense that the Psalms and the Canticles are poetry, it is nevertheless not prose. It is a kind of formal rhetoric of a rhythmic character which was used in the Christian meetings and had its background in Hellenistic and Hellenistic-Jewish liturgy.

When we consider the role of rhythmic verse in the New Testament after this survey it is not easy to generalize. We have found a variety of styles corresponding to a variety of formal traditions and to diverse settings. What is there in common between Jesus' balanced aphorisms employed in debate and the doxologies of Revelation? Different again are the exclamatory beatitudes and woes spoken out of militancy and persecution; or the confessions of faith couched in terms of astral symbolism.

We do well to remind ourselves that in any age poetry as an art has an immense variety of expressions. In the beginning of the Gospel the new world of meaning and discourse inevitably brought forth varieties of patterned speech, and some of these lyrical and visionary. In the Good News man's primal and childlike spontaneity was restored to him. If poetry is peculiarly the expression of man's psychic and affective life, it was to be expected that this new enlargement of language would include song and chant as well as new wisdom. When the dumb are cured in Scripture they not only speak but sing; just as when the crippled are healed they not only walk but leap.

The modern reader of poetry may naturally have questions about the poems we have been discussing. His criteria are drawn from our Western tradition in which sensuous richness, virtuosity of language, and the orchestration of many facets of experience are expected. If we think in terms of a sonnet of Keats or Wordsworth's *Prelude* or the work of Rilke or Yeats, we are evidently brought to a pause by such a different kind of poetry as we find in our canon. In a poem of John Donne or Yeats or Wallace Stevens the whole gamut of man's sensuous life is drawn upon, and an unlimited heritage from older cultures. By such standards the hymns and oracles of the New Testament will appear naïve if not insipid.

But we must bear in mind again the diversity of tongues and of rhetorical occasions. The naïve often has its own prestige in the arts as we know in the case of the primitive. The poetry of the New Testament, with some exceptions, can best be seen as the voice not of an established culture and sensibility, but of an iconoclastic moment and crisis in culture. Primitive Christian poetry is spoken, as it were, at the beginning of a world, indeed, at the beginning of the world. Its substance and forms are eloquent, then, of this hour, an hour, indeed, which ever renews itself for faith.

It has been said that so far as the graphic arts are concerned the

Early Church down to the third century had no images but rather signs. Thus the catacomb paintings afford us not a cultural language but signs, conventions that pointed to the redemption rather than symbolizing it. This is a misunderstanding. Yet early Christianity for a period fasted, so to speak, so far as concerns the symbolic wealth of paganism. So one can say that much of early Christian poetry is meagre in cultural and dramatic association. Yet to the believer the *naïveté* of the Canticles or the doxologies of Revelation have rhetorical power and not only because they are sacred texts. The experience of glory is more eloquent than that of beauty. The drama of redemption involves the imagination in a more compelling way than those of humanism. To the humanist the early Christian poetry may seem insipid, just as the Greek prose of the canon may seem plebeian to the classicist. Yet all such comparisons are misconceived. The first songs of Zion had their own universality. The arts of humanism testify incomparably to the hungers and passions and mystery of man, but he is the same man who in the Gospel passes through a narrow gate so that he may better order his own being. And, as we know, the *naïveté* of the early Christian speech came in course of time to wed itself to the cultures of the world and the conditions were so provided for the supreme poetry of Dante and of the Western imagination in all its prodigality.

VII

IMAGE, SYMBOL, MYTH

The study of the New Testament begins with
that of its tropes.

AUGUSTINE

THE PRECEDING CHAPTERS have dealt with the form and modes of the early Christian utterance. In every case and throughout we have seen how inseparable these were from the substance of the Gospel. *How* Jesus and his followers spoke and wrote could not be separated from what they communicated. It was the novelty of grace and the fundamental renewal of existence which brought forth a new fruit of the lips, new tongues and new rhetorical patterns. Such modulation of discourse was also conditioned by the changing theatres of the Christian activity. In each such new cultural setting the primal dynamic reshaped the particular language-world and language-vehicles to its own purposes and in its own defence.

I

But there is one aspect of the new speech that we have so far recognized only in an indirect way, and that is its metaphorical and symbolic character. If the Gospel was creative in a formal rhetorical aspect, it was also creative in all that has to do with image, symbol and myth. Here, too, the substance of the faith brought forth a new liberation of speech evident in its prodigality of imaginative vehicles. The language-phenomenon which broke into the world with the discourse of Jesus and which continued in the Church arose out of a depth of impulse which imposed plastic expression throughout. We cannot without qualification use such terms as 'poetic' or 'imaginative', since these terms today suggest aesthetic or romantic categories. The early Christian vision and grasp of existence, however, had a dynamic character, suggested by the formulas 'mythic mentality' and 'mythical ideation', a level of apprehension which the New Testament speaks of as that of the Spirit.

This aspect of the Gospel speech has already come before us at a number of points, especially in our attention to the early Christian poem. The cultic hymns and confessions which recite the cosmic career and victory of Christ evidently employ mythological legacies. Poetry in the Old Testament tradition has also been noted, carrying over not only the versification but the imagery of Israel. Strophic sayings assigned to Jesus rest on the pungent and figurative tradition of Israel's sages and prophets. Jesus' most down-to-earth rebukes and consolations had the kind of visionary concreteness which we know in an Amos or a Dante. Jesus could see the inexorable verdict of God on his generation in the image of a blasted fig tree, and the overcoming of indurated recalcitrance in the image of a mountain moved from its place. The prominence of story, parable and vision in the New Testament testifies to the mimetic and dramatic character of the early Christian witness; indeed, the narrative sections as a whole have often midrashic colouring and typological overtones required by the occasion. Even those considerable parts of the New Testament which may formally be classed as prose are rarely prosaic, and have their own connotative richness of meaning.

We shall do well before we go further to have before us the abundance of pictorial imagery used in the New Testament to set forth the Good News. This is employed in various ways to portray the events of salvation and their antecedents and outcomes: God's callings and visitations, man lost and found, the Redeemer and his work, the Judgment and the hereafter. To get before us the range and diversity of the material we can scan it topically. Thus spiritual beings are presented in figurative ways: God, Christ, Satan, antichrist, angels and demons; the *dramatis personae* of the divine epic: Adam, Noah, Abraham, Moses, Elijah, and the Second Adam. Events and divine acts and epochs, again, receive mythological statement: the beginning and end of things, the old and the new Israel or humanity, the turning-points of the world process identified with the flood, the migration of Abraham, the exodus and Mount Sinai; and above all the hinge of history represented by the Christ-drama or incarnation. In the case of so important a topic as that of the Christ we find a multitude of special dramatizations bearing on such matters as his origin, birth, baptism, temptation, transfiguration, cross, descent into Hell, Resurrection, ascension, Second Coming.

Or one can evoke the wealth of imagery by looking at the matter not in terms of topics but rather of literary forms, as we have already partly suggested. Here the gamut reaches from single metaphors and tropes through parables, allegories, visions, hymns, doxologies and oracles to extended mythological sections. A whole book like that of the Apocalypse comes to our attention here, and indeed, the Gospels themselves as wholes must be seen formally as cult-histories representing a unique mythological genre.

If we were viewing all this in the light of secular literary canons we would have to say that the New Testament writings are in large part works of the imagination, loaded, charged and encrusted with every kind of figurative resource and invention. The Apocalypse, again, is a masterpiece of surrealism. For the interpretation of its cumulative dramatic levels we may well call in the depth psychologists and the anthropologists as well as the modern literary critic. The Gospel of John offers a series of incomparable tableaux or unveilings; a sacred oratorio in which the minute particulars of a one-time moment of history have been sublimated as by a greater William Blake into a world-volume in whose flying leaves the fates of heaven and earth are portrayed. Again, for its part, a Gospel like that of Mark is a book of epiphanies, a tragedy yet not a tragedy, a sacred drama which culminates not in the death of a hero or a martyr—and as such appealing to our sense of pathos or admiration—but in a final austere transaction between God and men, carrying with it a reversal of the story of the race as hitherto understood.

Such is the rhetoric of the New Testament as viewed in its aspect of semantic mode and resources. Any fuller canvass would require attention also to the earlier wealth of imagery and myth of Israel so much drawn upon in the new language-impulse of emerging Christianity.

II

Rich and varied as is the use of metaphorical speech in the New Testaments, our attention is drawn first of all to those larger pictures which we can properly call mythological. Here is the structural symbol in which the first Christians represented the whole world-process from Alpha to Omega and in which they set forth the Gospel story. In short we have to do with myth, understood here in the sense of total world-representation, involving, of course, not only what we would call the external cosmos but man as well, and all in the light of God.

Now a paradox of biblical religion is that in both the Old Testament and in the New we have to do with faiths that are in a real sense iconoclastic, that is, mythoclastic. A chief feature of both is their rejection of pagan myth. Yet in both Testaments myth is overcome with the help of myth. The combated myths are drawn upon, transformed and purged. Old Testament prophecy was, indeed, sober over against the polytheism and the nature myths of the Baals, yet it set forth its own historical myth, not hesitating to employ dramatic traits borrowed from its rivals. In a similar way the men who gave us the New Testament employed the world pictures and the salvation pictures of their own time to set forth their faith. For the Word of God speaks with the words of men and with the everyday language of men. But the everyday words of men are image-words and the Word of God necessarily employs these.

We need to be reminded that in all cultures men live by images. The meaning of things, the coherence of the world, its continuities, values and goals, all these are established for the multitudes and for societies of men by this or that world-picture or mythos, with its associated emblems, archetypes, paradigms, fables, heroes, cults. Man's very being is affective and imaginative, and his powers of survival and creation are nourished by dynamic impulses which mediate themselves to him through inherited and ever-renewed dramatizations which define his world. Reason is implicit and diffused in his *mythos* and even when it orders itself as a conscious critical instrument it draws its vitality from the faith impulse associated with the myth-making faculty. If the Word of God must necessarily speak with the mythopoetic words of men, it is all the more inevitable that this should be so where the ultimate issues of existence are in question.

The early Christian Church was at grips in the presence of syncretism and Gnosticism with what has been called a 'riot of religious romanticisms', and it overcame this by its own sober Gospel appealing to the heart and to the will. Yet the Gospel went forth clothed with familiar imagery and myth indispensable for evoking the cosmic and cultural significance of the claims put forward. One has only to note how the New Testament Church presented the birth, death and significance of Christ or the significance of baptism and the Lord's Supper, by associating with these motifs drawn from Jewish and pagan syncretism of the time.

There has of late been a great deal of inconclusive discussion about the symbolic and mythological elements in the New Testament. It is inevitable that literalistic interpretation of the early Christian imagery should be challenged. The question then arises, however, as to what may be retained as valuable, true or historical. Can we translate the first-century epic of salvation—presented as it is in the ideas of that time and in the imaginative categories of that time— can we translate these into more contemporary language without loss?

Our purpose here is not to renew the whole question of miracles and the supernatural, or to deal extensively with the question of demythologizing the New Testament. What is to our purpose here is relevant to both, namely, to attend to the kind of plastic rhetoric produced by the new faith. We do, however, pause to make two points. A narrative miraculous in character is often the very best way to convey a mystery which may itself not be miraculous. When something is extraordinary there is a very human impulse to ascribe to it a miraculous character. This is the way we voice and evoke adequate wonder at what may indeed deserve wonder. Where we make our mistake is in attaching ourselves to the miraculous shell and losing the real wonder. Or, contrariwise, we can make the even worse mistake of dismissing the whole matter just because of the same confusion. All this applies to the kind of Christian imaginative and interpretative narrative represented in many of the miracles of or about Christ, including the birth stories and the Resurrection accounts. The birth stories, for example, appropriate wonderfully rich and familiar motifs expressive of the hunger of men for the Birth of the Divine Child, or the advent of the Prince of Peace, the dawn of the Golden Age, and in this way these stories convey the significance recognized by the Church in the coming of Christ. It is a mistake to factualize such imagery, whether as a condition for accepting it or rejecting it.

The second point to make is that as the world changes with the passage of time nothing except things like the multiplication table can be merely repeated without translation or interpretation. One cannot merely repeat the words of the Bible, or lay one passage of the New Testament next to another, and so pretend to communicate the Gospel. Even a translation of the Greek New Testament into English is an interpretation, just as the translation of Jesus' words into Greek was an interpretation and a change. Every good sermon fortunately is an interpretation. To merely reproduce the words of the New Testament is to falsify their original meaning and to defraud modern hearers of that meaning. To build a Gothic church in the second part of the twentieth century is an analogous error. This style to be understood presupposes a medieval mind and culture.

When it comes to the images and symbols and myths of the Bible we need to be discriminating. There is much variety here. Let us select such large pictures as those of Christ's descent from God and his return; or his deliverance of the new Israel from the law, flesh, sin and death; or the image of the Last Judgment. In such cases we cannot wisely carry the passage over into the different world of our own day *en bloc*. Their truth is linked with the outlook of the evangelists and the Early Church. Leaving aside the mistake of literalizing them, we should be at pains to put ourselves in the place of the writer and the first readers. How were these images understood then? Where does their main significance lie? But once this question is fairly met we shall already be on the way to that kind of understanding of them today which is not slavish and wooden.

III

We return then to the early Christian rhetoric in its aspects of symbol and imaginative power. And we have in view the more significant features—the terms in which redemption and judgment are presented—the way of conveying God's dealings with men. Jesus and his followers created a new speech in this sense also, that they quickened and revised the existing images by which men lived. The Gospel did, indeed, combat the myth of the time, but it also was a myth-making movement. One cannot say which came first, the eschatological sense of being at the embattled frontier between an old and a new world, or the imagery and *mythos* that reflected the experience and made it meaningful.

The Gospel arose out of that kind of radical break in human affairs when old customs and continuities are undermined; it reflected that level of experience in which man and the world are made and unmade, and in which language will inevitably have a dynamic character and inevitably take on symbolic or surreal expression. It is not surprising that Jesus speaks of Satan and of the angels, of the judgment drama and of the eschatological banquet. And it is not surprising that both he and the earliest Jewish Christian Church see all things in terms of dramatic supernatural struggle, of life through death, of the powers of the kingdom and of the Spirit of God. It is not surprising that Paul sees the life of the Christian and the Church as in a final phase of the struggle with the cosmic principalities and powers. In such a setting baptism is an awe-inspiring passage, and the Lord's Supper takes place in a preternatural setting of opposing forces, earthly and heavenly.

All this is only to make clear that the language of the New Testament has a large part of imaginative rhetoric, alone adequate to catch up the awareness and world-sense of the believers. The only way we can really understand it and communicate it is to enter into its original power. This can only be done as we identify ourselves with the original revelation and the original cause served, and witness to them in our own situation. Thus those perspectives open themselves up for us also which accompanied the original myth-making Gospel.

The Church needs to be sustained in all centuries by the original dynamic speech and conceptions, though their significance needs constantly to be quickened and rendered transparent anew. What constitutes Christian worship is always the transcendental dimension of insight and vision which is mediated through the world-transforming images, old and new. It is not a matter of escape or of a separate world of the sacred to which we are introduced by this or that inherited language of Zion. It is rather that the actual world and its always-threatening tyrannies of law, necessity, fate and compulsion, need constantly to be dispelled and overcome by faith, and particularly by that language of faith which certifies us of the true character of the world. Such images or myths are not a matter of world-view, in which we can be instructed, but a matter of the Spirit. In this sense, however, we can say that it is a matter of profound Christian orientation, of really knowing the way of the world as God rules it and overrules it. What is called for is that kind of *naïveté* in the good sense for which the realities of faith are indeed real, yet without escape from the common lot of men.

IV

If then we appreciate rightly the plastic and mythological character of much of the New Testament, we are not tempted to literalize it. We should not seek to reduce a painting to a blueprint, or to the canvas and pigments employed for it. The early Christian symbol, on the other hand, is not only 'poetry' in the sense of fancy or free-floating imagination. Rudolf Bultmann certainly recognizes its importance. He translates it into other categories, indeed—and this by no means involves a discarding of it. His categories seek to do justice to the word of the Cross.

But there is a basic question here. Do we move as he does from the pictorial and representational character of the myth to its supposed meaning for the heart alone? Or should we not recognize that the symbol, for all its imaginative and ancient character, yet tells us something Christian not only about ourselves but also about the visible world of time and space and about the work of God in a real world process? Our choice here rests in part upon our view of mythological language and cultural symbol, and our view as to what kind of truth they possess. Existentialism sees this truth as truth primarily about man. On this view the way in which we see the world tells us about ourselves, not about 'things' and the way things are and the way things happen. But this decision has enormous consequences for our view of the Christian life itself. The mythological portrayal in the New Testament of the whole story of man and salvation as the Bible presents it is, in effect, disparaged. In the Christian existentialist view of the Gospel such seemingly public matters as the history of God's people in the Old Testament, or the involvement of the Christ-drama in a human situation in Palestine in the time of Herod, or even the order of nature in which men live, all this is too easily subsumed or folded up into a profound God-man encounter. All that history represents is too easily telescoped into another kind of history of God and our freedom. Now what stands in the way of this loss of reality in the Gospel is the mythopoetic mode of the early Christian witness to these matters when its semantic character is rightly understood.

We should reckon with what we can learn about metaphorical and symbolic language from students of poetry: that it cannot really be translated, least of all into prose; that its meaning is to be thought in terms of its own distinctive mode of communication; that this kind of report of reality—as in a work of art—is more subtle and complex and concrete than in the case of a discursive statement, and therefore more adequate to the matter in hand and to things of importance.

When demythologizing is directed against literalism or against a dogmatic objectifying and secularizing of Christian faith and its images, we cannot but approve its aim. Faith should not be confused with acceptance of pictures of God's dealings taken as blueprints for belief, let alone credulity. But demythologizing fails to do justice to the meaning and truth in the imagery. In waiving the wisdom of the myth for a supposed more fundamental meaning in terms of encounter, it seems to be motivated by a radical despair with respect to the possibilities of human knowing and even of Christian knowing. In this scepticism all that understanding of the world and of the course of the world and of history which is imaged forth in the Christian revelation is surrendered as though of the order of fiction, and, indeed, as if it were a dangerous ideology. Demythologizing at this point appears to rest upon a sceptical legacy from the thought of Kant, perhaps enhanced by recent disillusionments in men's efforts to make sense of history. As a result all meaning is confined to an existentialist dimension. The recurrent formula here is that we can know the 'that' of revelation, but not its 'what' or 'how'. We can hear the Word but not see its meaning and working. At the root of all such forfeiture of meaning is a misunderstanding of the truth-aspect of Christian imagery and myth.

In seeking to understand the imagery we should also reckon with what we can learn from students of language in its social import. They tell us that the myths and ritual of tribes and peoples root back into man's dealings with the very conditions of existence. They have that kind of truth and reality which reflect hard-won experience, no doubt partial but validated by their role in group survival. The mysteries of man, world and time receive varying dramatic and mimetic formulation in language and action apart from which life is blind. Israel's deepened version of such readings of the world was unique in its grasp of man's moral being and his historical dimension. This provided the possibility for the Christian Gospel. The mythological representation of the course of the world in the New Testament is to be seen therefore as a new wisdom about man and God, based on Israel's experience, indeed, but corrected by that primordial re-creation of man to be identified with the crucifixion of Israel's truest representative.

What the early Christian faith meant, therefore, can only be grasped as we attend to its plastic language, giving full heed to what it meant in its original setting. The images of world redemption and judgment, of Messianic Banquet and Last Day, of the Birth of the Divine Child, of the turning of the water into wine, these images mean what they meant to the early witnesses in all their rich connotations. Our congenital modern demand that such language be rationalized must be resisted, as well as our readiness to put all such

forms of knowing out of court. Historical and critical study of the
material is by no means ruled out, and will only clarify its meaning,
granted that it is studied with recognition of its true character.
Transposition of the myth into provisional discursive or existential
analogies is desirable provided it be recognized that every such
formulation is a poor surrogate and must always again appeal back
to the original.

In varying ways and with varying degrees of significance the
symbol and myth of the New Testament instruct us as to aspects of
reality attained in the course of Israel's experience as taken up and
corrected and illuminated in the Christ-story. These pictorial
vehicles which served the evangelization of the Empire convey to us
a revealed understanding of such things as the life of men and
nations in time, the relation of Israel to other peoples and the
Church, the historical significance of Jesus of Nazareth, the way in
which God works in the world through situations and events, the
destiny of the individual and all creatures. In short the Christian
knows what the Gnostic vainly sought: who he is, whence he came,
whither he goes; especially because his relation to his fellow man and
to his place in life and in nature is better understood. The Christian
knows about his world and not only, as some existentialists seem
to hold, about his obligation. It is through images that all such
orientation of the believer in an enigmatic world is conveyed. The
world-understanding in question involves, of course, the heart as well
as the knowing faculties. But we should not moralize man's relation
to God as a creature in such a way as to exclude all relations to God
apart from the will.

We thus vindicate the intrinsic importance of the early Christian
rhetoric in its aspects of imagery. The new myth-making powers of
the Christian movement meant more than an overthrow of rival
myths and more than a liberation from letter and from law. It meant
the portrayal of the real nature of things and of the course of existence
so far as human speech could encompass such mysteries. Comparing
lesser things with greater, we appropriate the myth and symbol of
the New Testament by opening ourselves to its wisdom in the same
order of response with which we encounter art or read poetry.
Though this order of knowing is closer to that of ancient spell or
visionary realization, or the world-making of the child, yet it is, for
this very reason, a total and immediate kind of knowing and one
that involves us totally.

Our attention to the metaphorical aspect of the earliest Christian speech in this chapter has added an essential perspective to our grasp of that rhetoric as a whole. We have seen that the Gospel represented a new outburst and plenitude of human utterance and communication in all aspects of language. Language is so primordial a gesture of living things that any radical renewal of it such as the one we have documented points to an epoch-making moment in the human story. The early Christian consciousness of this break in culture comes to expression in its eschatological imagery as well as in its novel speech-forms. The grasp upon ultimate reality coincident with this revolution in speech constituted no less than a new *genus homo*, and one capable therefore of unprecedented moral energies and cultural creativity. It has been said that no peoples have a history in the true sense except Israel and those that have entered into its understanding of man. The reality-sense of other human groups is prehistorical and prepersonal by comparison. With Christianity the self-understanding of man broke through into universality and the new speech that accompanied this event signalled no less than what was claimed by the early witnesses, namely, a new creation.

INDEXES

INDEX OF NAMES

INDEX OF REFERENCES

Papias 40

Hippolytus
94, 103

Clem. Alex.
Prot. IX,
84   109 f.

Jerome
Ep. 22   12

NEW TESTAMENT APOCRYPHA, ETC.

*Acts of Paul and
Thecla*
3   38

*Coptic Gospel of
Thomas,*
saying
51   49

Letter of Eugnostos
49
Jesu Christi Sophia
49